I0839802

The bane of humankind is the malignant lie, employed by the malevolent liar for depraved self-interest, in politics and families. The ability to initiate and sustain the lie takes no special talent nor intellect, only the capacity to abandon personal integrity and character.

When good people try to correct the mendacity, the liar gets angry and vindictive. So the question is, in politics and families: Roll over in silent acquiescence or stand up for truth and take the hit?

ALSO BY
TOM ERSIN

————

From Dysfunction to Resilience:
A Good Road to Travel

Trumpism:
Why Traditional Republicans Should Withdraw Support [2017-2021: A Primer]

Trump's Last Year in Office:
Two Impeachments and 400,000 Funerals

Trump's Presidency:
A Real-Time Commentative History [2019-2021]

Trump's Presidency:
A Real-Time Commentative History [2017-2019]

Barack vs. the Anti-PC:
Laying the Groundwork for a 2016 Donald Trump Presidential Run

My Election 2008 Email Wars:
Disinformation Before Social Media Ubiquity

TRUMP'S FIRST YEAR IN OFFICE:

The Awakening

TOM ERSIN

GraniteWord.com
Troy, Michigan

Print Edition ISBN: 9798862597851

Written and edited by Tom Ersin (tom@graniteword.com)

Printed in the United States of America

Front Cover Photo ("Donald Trump"): JStone/Shutterstock.com

Cover Design by: Tom Ersin

20240307

GraniteWord.com
Troy, MI

<div align="center">~~~</div>

Please Make This Author Happy

I hope you enjoy reading this book as much as I did writing it. I'd be forever appreciative if you would post a review on Amazon. Just a sentence or two and a rating would be great. Reviews are lifeblood for authors and they help readers find my books.

(https://www.amazon.com/dp/B0CJXGRXL2)

Thanks a lot,
Tom

My Free Gift for You

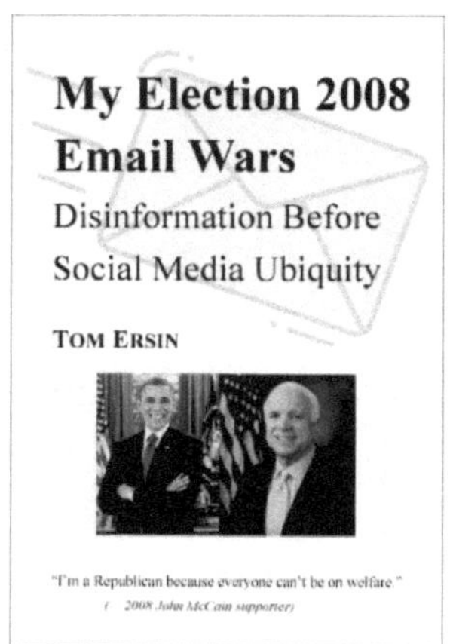

Download for FREE: *My Election 2008 Email Wars: Disinformation Before Social Media Ubiquity*

Join my email newsletter and get this e-book about conspiracy theories at the voter level before social media was a thing. This book can be downloaded to your computer and read there or transferred to any e-reader.

Download this e-book for free today at:

https://graniteword.com/free-book-my-election-2008-email-wars-2020/

This Series

This is the second in my subseries comprising the three books:

Trumpism: Why Traditional Republicans Should Withdraw Support [2017-2021: A Primer]

Trump's First Year in Office: The Awakening

Trump's Last Year in Office: Two Impeachments and 400,000 Funerals

All three books listed above are carve-outs from my exhaustive 1,400-page history:

Trump's Presidency: A Real-Time Commentative History [2017-2019]

Trump's Presidency: A Real-Time Commentative History [2019-2021]

This book, *Trump's First Year in Office: The Awakening,* is the second volume in the subseries, all drawn from the perspective of a long-time avid political observer. Think of the histories as an in-depth every-Thursday recap of all the news you were too busy to consume because you had a life and didn't realize the gravity of the dysfunction and disinformation. When you see my opinion you'll know it. Much more often, when you see facts, quotations, and details, I'm assuring you that I've backed up their accuracy with careful research and citation.

TABLE OF CONTENTS

IBATR: Your Critical Thinking Primer

This book resides on a foundation of *critically thoughtful communication*. This is communication that consistently incorporates the principles of critical thinking and best supports the ethical, accurate transfer of information.

It does not involve intellectual hoop-jumping or mental gymnastics that only lawyers, philosophers, or Mensa members understand. It's a simple form of critical thinking that anyone should use to cut through the adult male bovine excreta and get to the most accurate possible version of the truth regarding any given issue or question.

IBATR (pronounced *"EYE-batter"*) is the acronym representing the five legs of our critically thoughtful communication table. When even one leg is broken — or missing — the table wobbles. Milk spills.

> *I) Information* — Carefully consider the communicated information or question at hand, ensuring you understand it clearly. Assign no immediate favoritism toward information sources and no immediate judgment about accuracy or inaccuracy of the information.

> *B) Biases* — Examine all biases you or the sources might have surrounding the communicated information or question at hand.

> *A) Assumptions* — Examine all assumptions you or the sources might have surrounding the communicated information or question at hand.

T) Truth — Maintain a commitment to truth and honesty, and consider the level of this commitment for each communication or information source.

R) Response — Carefully draw a conclusion and formulate a response. And always remember that this might require modification based upon new analysis, new communication, or new information-source evaluation.

IBATR is the Holy Grail of successful communication. Granted, perfection is not possible. But applying one's best intentions *is* possible. Applied IBATR best intentions means that we try to follow the steps to the best of our ability. And the last one, Step "R," always allows for the reexamination of information, sources, and personal motives.

Critically thoughtful communication and IBATR constitute the trunk of the communications tree. When this trunk is weakened, branches break or die — or get misquoted. This acronym represents the foundation of accurate, ethical information exchange. Make this acronym your best friend. Put aside time for it. When it is speaking to you, give it your full attention as if it were the most important acronym on Earth. Compliment it now and then on a new hypothesis (or hairstyle). Surprise your acronym occasionally with an intimate rendezvous at home. And never, *ever*, dispute your acronym when the two of you are with friends.■

Introduction

After Election Day, Nov. 8, 2016, I was in a depressive funk for a month or so along with half the electorate. Immediately after Inauguration Day the excrement started hitting the machine creating airflow: ridiculous, petty lies about inaugural crowd size; disrespect of fallen CIA members in front of their memorial; censorship of EPA employees; haphazard, illegal Muslim travel ban; epithets for U.S. senators and judges. The list could fill books — and it has.

By May 17, 2017, the Justice Department had been presented with enough evidence to warrant the appointment of former 12-year FBI director and unassailable person of integrity Robert S. Mueller III (Republican) as special counsel. The special counsel was commissioned that day to investigate possible conspiracy between the Trump campaign and Russian nationals to influence illegally the 2016 United States presidential election in then-candidate Trump's favor. You might remember hearing about Donald famously responding to the news of Mr. Mueller's appointment: "This is the end of my presidency. I'm f***ed!"

From Day 1, consuming political news became "like drinking out of a firehose," to quote *CNN* anchor Don Lemon. By July 2017 I decided I needed to create a record of this presidency. Using my online magazine (don't call it a blog), *GraniteWord.com*, I started writing a commentative, observational summary of developments each week without fail until Mr. Trump finished his term.

Do I have opinions? Yes. And I share them often. But more prominent in my comprehensive content is the factual recording of unfolding events. This book charts the first year of Trump's presidency from the perspective of an avid (compulsive?), long-time political news consumer. Think of it as an in-depth every-Thursday recap of all the news you were too busy to consume because you had a life and didn't realize the gravity of the dysfunction and corruption. It's all here in one place. When you see my opinion you'll know it. Much more often, when you see facts, quotations, and details, I'm assuring you that I've backed up their accuracy with careful research and citation.

The Beginning

06/16/2015 — Donald Trump announces run for U.S. president

05/26/2016 — Donald Trump clinches Republican presidential nomination

11/08/2016 — Election Day: Donald Trump defeats Hillary Clinton

01/20/2017 — Inauguration Day: Donald Trump takes office as 45th U.S. President

05/17/2017 — Special Counsel Robert Mueller is appointed by DOJ to investigate Trump-Russia 2016 election interference, conspiracy, and obstruction of justice

07/04/2017 — In the spirit of the patriotic holiday, author tells self, "I gotta start writin' this stuff down."

07/26/17 — Opening Article: Second Continental Congress, 45th President, and IBATR

Critical Thinking

Critical thinking. Rhetoric. Persuasion. Argument. Civility. These words used to carry weight. They used to *mean* somethin' (— *thanks to Drunk Uncle, aka Bobby Moynihan, "Saturday Night Live"*). The concepts were hashed out in the days of Aristotle (student of Plato), Quintillion (student of Cicero), and Dr. Philato (student of Oprahmetrius). They are the foundation upon which communication through language rests.

On July 4 we celebrated Independence Day, declared in 1776 by the Second Continental Congress during which critical thought, persuasion, and communication again were stretched to their fullest potential and produced the birth of a nation.

But critical thinking is not just for Founding Fathers anymore.

IBATR

To review, IBATR (pronounced *"EYE-batter"*) comprises my simplified steps representing the five legs of our critically thoughtful communication table. When even one leg is broken — or missing — the table wobbles. Milk spills.

> 1) **Information:** Carefully consider and understand the *information*. Assign no immediate judgment about the content or source.

> 2) **Bias:** Examine all *bias* — yours and the source's.

3) **Assumptions:** Examine all *assumptions* — yours and the source's.

4) **Truth:** Commit to *truth* and honesty. Examine the source's commitment.

5) **Response:** Formulate a fair, civil *response*, and reexamine when necessary.

This brings us to *persuasion*. The skillful use of this powerful tool (weapon?) carries an ethical responsibility, i.e., it should incorporate the principles of IBATR. Aristotle (the Stephen Colbert of his day) was concerned about the misuse of persuasion, which is why he and his Greek buds specified certain ethical requirements as being indispensable to the art and science of rhetoric (aka communication and persuasion).

The ethical speaker or writer must be "a [person] of good intentions … and dedicated to truth, accuracy, and goodwill [civility]" — not to mention exhibiting "fair-mindedness" and "credibility." (Memering, Dean & Palmer, William; *Critical Thinking: Discovering How to Compose and Analyze Arguments;* 2006.)

Trump Logic

Thomas Jefferson and John Adams would have killed to have audio and video in their day. To be able to confront a rhetorical adversary with an indisputable record of what that adversary said, as he denies ever saying it, would be a perfect (rhetorical) world.

Alas, welcome to 2017. Audio and video are fun toys. But for 40% or so of the electorate and most elected Republicans, audio and video records have no meaning, no connection to their "logical" reality. The 40% or so believe the lies and denials and eat up the incivility, video evidence be damned. Elected Republicans look the other way and give tacit approval for the lying, denying, and boorishness.

Donald Trump is an uncivil rhetorical anomaly that even Aristotle and Thomas Jefferson might never have contemplated. As has been widely reported, Mr. Trump has no shame; he cannot be embarrassed by being caught in a lie. He simply responds by adding another one to the onslaught. *Argumentum verbosium* is logical fallacy by avalanche of plausible-sounding arguments too laborious to untangle. President Trump operates in a constant state of what I call *prevaricatum verbosium:* logical fallacy by avalanche of mendacity too voluminous to remember.

I don't know if critical thinking and IBATR will protect our country through the era of Trump, but it's the only thing we have. Well, we have the law. But the lack of IBATR and use of unethical persuasion drives those who control the applicable laws — currently GOP congressional committee leaders and members. That brings us back to rhetoric and critical thought. It's all we have; we can't give up on it.

The next time Donald Trump says, "The [inaugural] audience was the biggest ever"; "The Pew reports ... show voter fraud"; "[I'll] save ... Medicaid ... without cuts ... have to do it"; "She was bleeding from her face-lift, or wherever"; "The mainstream media is all fake news" — the next time he says stuff like this, ask yourself if Mr. Trump is "a person of good intentions ... and dedicated to truth, accuracy, and goodwill." Is he "fair-minded"? Is he "credible"? *(— thanks to Aristotle)*

Contrary to White House deputy press secretary Sarah Huckabee Sander's recent up-is-down regurgitation of President Trump's sentiments, *CNN* is not fake news. At the end of last June it retracted a story linking Trump ally Anthony Scaramucci to a Russian investment fund. *CNN* made a mistake, then made a distinctly *un*-fake news correction by issuing a retraction and firing three journalists responsible for the inaccurate story. The Trump administration castigated *CNN* for this act of responsible journalism. Now which one is "dedicated to truth, accuracy, and goodwill"?∎

08/06/17 — No, Sen. Jeff Flake, You Did NOT Do Enough

Random House just released Arizona Republican Sen. Jeff Flake's new book, *Conscience of a Conservative*. One hundred forty pages for $27. How does he get away with that? We'll see if it sells. Let's analyze his potential sales pool. In the book, Flake trashes President Trump. There's one Amazon purchase out the window. He also severely chastises his fellow GOP legislators and other party movers and shakers for enabling The Donald to political victory. Many more units left in back stock. But as reviewers and critics have pointed out, Flake has voted with President Trump about 94% of the time. Right there he loses the popular vote by about 2.86 million sales (though he still could make a profit in the Electoral College).

Remembering Barry Goldwater

Sen. Flake is a self-described Barry Goldwater conservative, hence the title of his book, which he borrowed from Goldwater's 1960 work of the same name. Flake wants the Republican Party to return to its conservative, Goldwater-y roots of promoting free markets, limited government, and a strong defense. Two out of three?

It's interesting to note that Barry Goldwater had a libertarian pro-choice stance regarding abortion. He also supported President Bill Clinton's efforts to stop the exclusion of gays from military service. I wonder where the Mormon conservative Jeff Flake stands on those issues. Here are a few other insights into the Goldwater state of mind:

> "I don't understand this incivility. I don't understand why the religious right is dominating the Republican Party."

(Goldwater, Barry; R-Ariz.; former U.S. senator; 1994; as cited in Dean, John W.; *Conservatives Without Conscience;* 2006.)

"I will fight [the radical right] every step of the way if they try to dictate their moral convictions to all Americans in the name of conservatism."

(Goldwater, Barry; R-Ariz.; U.S. senator; floor speech; *Congressional Record;* 9/16/1981.)

"Politics and governing demand compromise."

(Goldwater, Barry; R-Ariz.; former U.S. senator; 1994; as cited in Dean, John W.; *Conservatives Without Conscience;* 2006.)

Jeff Flake — Now

Maybe Mr. Flake is on to something. "Governing demands compromise." "I don't understand this incivility." "I will fight [the radical right] every step of the way." Even liberal Democrats can get on board with these sentiments. Sure, Sen. Flake seems to align with Donald Trump on *policy,* but his most scathing criticism of the president is aimed at Trump's *character:* the suffocating narcissism, the lying, immaturity, volatile unpredictability, misogyny, racism, xenophobia, blatant self-promotion, massive conflict of interest as president and real estate billionaire, philosophical incoherence … Jeff, you had me at *suffocating narcissism.* I'm not sure if Flake used all those terms in his book. If he missed any they can go in the sequel.

Sen. Flake writes, "We pretended that the emperor wasn't naked. Even worse: We checked our critical faculties at the door and pretended that the emperor was making sense." To his credit, Jeff Flake was a Never Trumper from before the primaries through the election.

Jeff Flake — Back When

But where was Jeff Flake during the lead-up to Trump's political rise, during President Obama's first and second term? Where was Jeff Flake while the GOP tacitly was encouraging tea party racism, nativism, and obstreperous anti-Obama lies?

Mr. Flake rightly calls out Newt Gingrich and his scorched-earth politics of personal destruction. Good for him. But where was Jeff when Newt was espousing his brand of not-so-subtle dog-whistled racism?

> "[I don't know] whether he needs large amounts of rest [or] whether he needs to go play basketball for a while. ... I'm assuming there's some rhythm to Barack Obama that the rest of us don't understand."
>
> (Gingrich, Newt, R-Ga., 2012 presidential primary candidate, former U.S. House speaker; *Fox News' On the Record* with Greta Van Susteren; 9/25/2012.)

> "Obama knows how to make the United States look like Detroit, [while I know how to make it] look like Houston."
>
> (Gingrich, Newt, R-Ga., 2012 presidential primary candidate, former U.S. House speaker; *Fox News' The Sean Hannity Show*; 5/10/2011.)

As a Detroit boy I'm particularly bothered by that last insinuation.

Why wasn't then-congressman Jeff Flake on *Meet the Press* lambasting Gingrich for his consistent racist jabs during Obama's 2012 reelection campaign?

Speaking of *Meet the Press*, Sen. Flake defended himself this week by saying he personally did enough to stand up to the bogus "birtherism" conspiracy, which made Donald Trump a Republican star. Without Trump's full-court birther press and consequent notoriety before and after the 2012 election, there would be no *President* Trump. I'm sorry — I watch a lot of political cable news. I especially was enthralled during the 2012 campaign. I have no recollection of congressman and 2012 senatorial candidate Flake speaking out against Trump's despicable racist conspiracy theories. I'm sorry, Jeff — you did *not* do enough. You are right that your party was wrong. But you did not speak out enough.

And where was Jeff Flake when Romney campaign Co-Chair John Sununu was broadcasting his dog-whistled remarks?

"He's lazy" (referring to President Obama).

(Sununu, John, R-N.H., 2012 Romney-Ryan presidential campaign co-chair, former [George H. W. Bush] White House chief of staff, former governor; *MSNBC's Andrea Mitchell Reports;* 10/4/2012.) *(a shocked Andrea asked John if he wanted to qualify this remark; he did not)*

"When you're not that bright, you can't get better prepared" (referring to President Obama).

(Sununu, John, R-N.H., 2012 Romney-Ryan presidential campaign co-chair, former [George H. W. Bush] White House chief of staff, former governor; *Fox News;* 10/4/2012.)

Where was Jeff Flake when Sarah Palin and Michele Bachmann were putting in their two bigoted cents?

"President Obama's shuck and jive shtick with these Benghazi lies must end."

> (Palin, Sarah, R-Alaska, former governor, 2008 [John
> McCain] vice presidential candidate; Facebook post;
> as cited in *The Washington Post*; 10/24/2012.)

> "Now we've moved into the realm of [Obama's] 'gangster
> government.'"

> (Bachmann, Michele, R-Minn., U.S. representative;
> floor speech; 7/11/2009.)

Finally, where was Jeff Flake when the other myriad lies about President Obama and his policies were flying, heavily supported by the tea party: lies about death panels, health care rationing, socialized medicine, gun confiscation, socialized auto industry, doubling the deficit, making the economy worse, and on, and on?

Too Little, too Late

Donald Trump did not rise to the presidency on his good looks (or manners). The Republican Party made a deal with the devil after Barack Obama's 2008 election. In return for tea party support of anti-Obama obstructionism, the GOP looked the other way and gave tacit approval to race-baiting and xenophobia. The colossal mendacity and lack of critical thinking was astonishing. Donald saw his opening and Republican leaders ultimately lost their influence. And forget *tacit*. Trump openly cheered the rampant intolerant nativism, nihilism, and anti-PC hatred. The base cheered him back and he took over their party.

Sen. Flake, your book is nice and all but it's too little, too late for this administration. You did *not* do enough when it mattered, when this debacle still could have been prevented. We'll see if you have accomplished anything that might prevent the next Trump-like joker from commandeering your party and becoming president.■

08/10/17 — Fire and Fury, and Frankly Power (Ooh, "FRANKLY" Power!)

[TOPICS: North Korea]

"North Korea best not make any more threats to the United States … [or] they will be met with fire and fury, and frankly power, the likes of which this world has never seen before."

> (Trump, Donald, R-N.Y., U.S. president; news conference; Trump National Golf Club, Bedminster, N.J.; 8/8/2017.)

"We had the biggest audience in the history of inaugural speeches."

> (Trump, Donald, R-N.Y., U.S. president; interview conducted by Muir, David; *ABC News;* 1/25/2017.)

"I watched when the World Trade Center came tumbling down. And I watched in Jersey City, New Jersey, where thousands and thousands of people were cheering as that building was coming down. Thousands of [Arabs] were cheering."

> (Trump, Donald, R-N.Y., presidential primary candidate; campaign speech; Birmingham, Ala.; 11/21/2015.)

"There's no records! There's no records! There's no birth certificate! There's no records!"

(Trump, Donald, R-N.Y., presidential candidate tease; *Fox News' On the Record* with Greta Van Susteren; 4/11/2011.) *(referring to President Obama's existence)*

President Salesman

These are just a few of the multitudinous instances of Donald Trumpian lies. They go back decades. We've known who this person is for a long time.

The dictator Kim Jong Un always has had access to American news even though he allows none to the North Korean people. So what makes President Trump think Kim will take seriously the president's latest, improvised superlative-alicious statement in the wake of hundreds of blusterous, mendacious Trumpian pronouncements?

Of course an unwanted result of our president's narcissistic cluelessness and incessant hot air is that even if Kim Jong Un assumes Trump's threat is an empty one, it still could anger the petulant madman (Kim, that is) to initiate a deadly response.

Trump Has His Cake ...

Donald simply cannot turn off his sleazy, snake-oil-salesman persona. Even while boasting on national TV about his international diplomacy skills — employed during dessert conversation with Chinese President Xi Jinping about the April 2017 U.S. retaliation against Syria for using chemical weapons — Trump could not help himself. He had to inject that the (Trump private country club) Mar-a-Lago piece of chocolate cake President Xi was enjoying was "the most beautiful piece of chocolate cake that you've ever seen." And of the 59 unmanned missile strikes, Trump gushed again to *Fox*

Business Network's Maria Bartiromo: "It's so incredible. It's brilliant. It's genius."

Now I'm guessing Kim Jong Un knows beautiful chocolate cake — the greatest imperial chocolate cake that North Korean presidential palace pastry chefs can prepare. Because if it's not the best, chefs die. (Are we clear? Crystal?) So right there Kim knows Trump is lying. And if he'll lie about cake, it's just a short jump to lying about bringing "fire and fury, and frankly power, the likes of which this world has never seen before."

If "fire and fury" initially were not enough to convince Kim Jong Un of the gravity of his potential actions against the U.S., the American president repeated the fire-and-fury threat, but the second time added "and *power*, the likes of which ..." yada, yada. Additionally President Trump modified the word *power* with the amplifier *frankly*. Take that, Kim!

To clarify, Donald *wasn't* being frank about the "fire and fury," but he really meant it when he said "power." Everyone knows when a politician puts the word *frankly* before another word or declaration, they *really* mean it, contrary to everything they said before the word *frankly*, which they didn't really mean, or at least were wishy-washy about.

... And, Frankly, Lies About It, Too

All seriousness aside, President Trump's words carry little-to-no weight. Frankly, he lies — a lot. Democrats always knew it. Independents now know it. Most Republican legislators secretly admit it. Heck, even his base knows it, but in their no-account, no-accountability fantasy world, Trump's lying is a badge of honor.

The real problem, however — at least with foreign policy — is that the *world* knows the current U.S. president is a chronic fabulist. He lies 95% of the time. But ironically the 5% truth-telling is the kicker, the danger. Is he truly ignorant enough to consider raining "fire and fury" down upon North Korea in a preemptive attack? There's a 95% chance he's lying about the seriousness of this threat, as Kim also knows. But it's that 5% chance of veracity that could kill us all.

Or he could be lying now but change his mind later based upon a *Fox News* retweet or in reaction to special counsel Robert Mueller closing in on him with the Russia investigation. You see, Donald Trump not only lies, he's incompetent, impetuous, and capable of risking hundreds of thousands of lives to do some dog-wagging.

This is no joke: President Trump must be removed from office before large numbers of innocent people die. Until then we have to trust the generals to rein him in. And in all future elections we absolutely must heed the advice of Maya Angelou — or Oprah Winfrey, or Oprah's intern, no one knows for sure: "When someone shows you who they are, believe them, the first time." ∎

08/17/17 — President Trump Has No Bottom; It Will Get Worse

[TOPICS: Charlottesville neo-Nazi "Unite the Right" rally]

Last Week

Remember last week when the worst thing we had to fear from President Trump's bombastic ineptitude was nuclear war on the Korean Peninsula? Ahh, the good old days: Donald's schoolyard taunts while brandishing the nuclear football; snappy comebacks from Pyongyang's Dear Leader about wiping out Guam and other parts of Earth; and some random Trumpian threats of Argentinian invasion and nation building thrown in for good measure.

If you thought it couldn't get any worse, you haven't been paying attention. We've had scads of it-can't-get-any-worse moments since the president announced his candidacy. But it always does — get worse, that is.

Last Year

Reminisce to Nov. 9, 2016, the day after Election Day, when you were surprised by how many of your social media "friends" ventured out of the pro-Trump closet. All of a sudden you had previously-thought-to-be-reasonable people posting about, "OK, we need to give the guy a chance. He's our president now."

Of course I was one of those who said, "NO! We DON'T give the guy a chance! We already know how badly he will perform! He has let us know that in voluminous ways!" And my social media contacts knew I was serious because I normally hate exclamation points. I also lost a few friends when I pointed out that even if they as Trump supporters are not racist, they have accepted Trump's racism and tacitly approve of it.

Of all the "Make America Great Again" ranters, I only defriended one person, a literal friend, who could not stop posting hateful, vicious alt-right vitriol usually involving the Pepe (cartoon character) icon. I continued arguing with the rest of them until it became old.

This Week

This week Donald Trump has emboldened white nationalists and encouraged the start of a race war. If you think it can't get any worse, you're still wrong. But we are at the president's current nadirian extreme.

Here's a brief timeline:

— FRIDAY NIGHT —

Nazis, white supremacists, and alt-righters — in Tiki-torch formation chanting hateful slogans — are gathered at the site of the Charlottesville, Virginia, Confederate statue of Robert E. Lee slated to be decommissioned (by popular vote).

— SATURDAY —

Amid other violence, a 20-year-old alleged neo-Nazi rams his car into a crowd of counterprotesters (the good guys), killing Heather Heyer and injuring about 19 others.

— SATURDAY NIGHT —

President Trump appears on television to condemn "hatred, bigotry, and violence on many sides" without mentioning Nazis, the KKK, or white supremacists.

— MONDAY —

President Trump bows to steep internal and external pressure to say the right thing. He reads a stiff-as-a-board statement verbatim from his teleprompter condemning the KKK, neo-Nazis, white supremacists, and hatred as "evil … [and] repugnant to everything we hold dear as Americans."

— TUESDAY —

In a combative news conference, President Trump essentially takes back his condemnation and equates activists protesting racism with the neo-Nazis and white supremacists who threatened and killed over the weekend. He defended the Nazis and KKK as having been the ones with the legal permit to protest, and he repeated the false equivalency that there was "violence [and fine people] on both sides." He invented a new term, the *alt-left*, to describe a nonexistent group and further prop up his falsely equivalent argument. White supremacist icons Richard Spencer, David Duke, and *The Daily Stormer* signaled they were encouraged and heartened by the president's remarks.

Donald Trump's presidency is in mortal danger of collapse, but he doesn't seem concerned. Everybody and their brother including many GOP legislators and leaders have condemned Trump's equivocation and apparent honest expression of his true racist beliefs. Nazis, the KKK, and other components of the alt-right support him and he supports them. As many pundits have noted, condemning Nazis is the easiest thing in the world for an American politician to do, but Trump can't put his heart into it.

Republicans also are receiving heavy criticism including from their own. Though they condemn the KKK, Nazis, and alt-right, they won't mention (let alone disavow) Trump by name and they continue to support his presidency. They continue to be invertebrate.

There is only one thing to do: We must pressure the GOP to demand the president's resignation. Top administration people must leave. All of government must refuse to work with the man until he resigns. Sure, it's never been done before. But there never has been any president like Donald Trump. (I mean that in a bad way.) This is not Trump's bottom. After many a "new low" it's clear that Trump has no bottom.

"I told you so" only goes so far. It doesn't solve any problems. And it's immature. But I'm fondly anticipating November rolling around this year. That's when I'll be looking for those "See Your 1-Year Memories" notifications from Facebook. I should have a good stream of sharable memory posts saying things like, "I'm terrified of a Trump presidency"; "Check back in a year to see if we should have just given the guy a chance"; and "Talk to me next year and we'll see, 'How bad can it can get?'"

————————

On a profoundly serious note, our deepest sympathies go out to the families of Lt. H. Jay Cullen and Trooper-pilot Berke M. M. Bates, the Virginia state troopers killed in the helicopter accident while monitoring the Unite the Right gathering in Charlottesville, Virginia. And sincerest of condolences to the family of Heather Heyer, the 32-year-old Caucasian woman who lost her life at the same event while counterprotesting neo-Nazis, white supremacists, the KKK, and other groups that are part of the self-described alt-right.

Heather Heyer, by ethnicity and birth, would have been protected and well treated under the alt-right philosophy. But she protested to protect the rights of all citizens, realizing that the mistreatment of one is the mistreatment of all. Never before has one of Heather's favorite maxims meant more: "If you're not outraged, you're not paying attention."

Update to Timeline

"Sad to see the history and culture of our great country being ripped apart with the removal of our beautiful statues
and monuments. You … can't change history, but you can
learn from it. Robert E Lee, Stonewall Jackson - who's next,
Washington, Jefferson? So foolish! Also … the beauty that is
being taken out of our cities, towns and parks will be greatly
missed and never able to be comparably replaced!"

(Trump, Donald, R-N.Y., U.S. president; Twitter
posts; 8/17/2017).■

08/24/17 — Teleprompter Trump vs. Wing-It Trump

The Barron

Don't you feel sorry for 11-year-old Barron Trump? No, I'm not talking about being upbraided by the Tucker Carlson-founded *Daily Caller* for dressing like a kid instead of a Cabinet member. I'm talking about in six or eight years. Imagine Barron in 12th grade American History class when the teacher covers the key points about our 45th president: 1) unanimously considered the worst U.S. president by historians; 2) forced from office within a year of inauguration to avoid Russian collusion and obstruction of justice convictions; 3) set race and gender relations back decades; 4) consistently embarrassed America on the world stage; and 5) cemented Richard Nixon's status as the *second*-most corrupt president ever to serve.

Sure, Barron will be wealthy beyond belief, but he'll have to live down his family legacy for the rest of his life. Now there's a juxtaposition: a lifetime of riches alongside a lifetime of shame. Don Jr., Ivanka, and Eric have been complicit and deserve to share in the disgrace. But young Barron has no choice. I feel bad for him. Let's hope Melania puts a little more effort into that campaign to fight cyberbullying.

The Two Donalds

The Donald has two settings: Teleprompter Trump and Wing-It Trump (Jennifer Rubin of *The Washington Post* calls the latter "Crazy Trump"). Teleprompter Trump speaks in complete sentences with little veracity or flare. Wing-It Trump speaks in stream-of-consciousness snippets and nuggets also with little veracity but lots of flare. Wing-It Trump, however, offers an accurate look into the man's soul. And as anyone who's been paying attention knows, it's not pretty.

There was an incredibly clear juxtaposition (good word) of the two Donalds in his appearances over the past two days. On Monday Teleprompter Trump made a presidential address to the nation outlining his Afghanistan policy. You always can tell Teleprompter Trump by the way he pivots robotically back and forth between his left and right script screens. Can't this guy take some time away from golf and cable news to learn how to use a teleprompter? His eyes are laser-locked on either screen for the allotted five to 10 sentences each. It's embarrassing.

The Afghanistan address was a hurried event, moved up to draw attention away from the president's Charlottesville debacle last week during which he gave cover to Nazis. Aww, I guess that's not fair — they were *neo*-Nazis. Pundits have pointed out that Vice President Mike Pence was rushed back early from an overseas trip to attend Trump's address. If it wasn't rushed, pundits asked, why didn't they stick to their originally scheduled day sometime after Pence's originally scheduled return home?

President Trump apparently fooled many people during his vague policy address. There was little change from Obama's Afghanistan policy except to add vagueness. Did I mention the speech was vague? Republicans, hoping for any hint of sanity, respectability, or maturity, praised the address as "long overdue" and "better than nothing."

I'm kidding. Many called it "measured" and "presidential." But for all the perfume chief of staff John Kelly poured over this pig, Trump still got some wing-it-esque nuggets into his speech. He said he's "a problem-solver." The military audience's mental snickering was deafening. He called terrorists "losers" — again. He said, "We will learn from history." Except that's one thing Trump *doesn't* do — the speechwriters have a sense of irony. Trump also said he's "studied this problem from every angle." But that's not speechwriters' irony. That's just plain fibbing.

The Contradiction

But there is one overwhelming contradiction that stood out to me. The president described how he initially wanted to go with his instincts (which he said he historically does) and simply pull up stakes in Afghanistan, lock, stock, and Mother-of-All-Bombs barrel. But he listened to his generals. Mr. Trump said he changed his mind about his long-time Afghanistan stance because "all of my life, I heard that decisions are much different when you sit behind the desk in the Oval Office."

If he's heard (and apparently realized) that decisions are different when one is president, Why didn't he ever consider that before bellowing the many stupid policy statements he has made over the last decade, especially while trashing President Obama? Well he *did* consider it — but decided to lie instead. He's known this all along. But the lies made him famous.

Teleprompter Trump went on to criticize Obama's handling of the Iraq-Afghanistan wars, saying he made wrong decisions about things Trump would have done differently. But President Trump also never acknowledges (when lying) that conditions, and knowledge of conditions, change over time. Trump said he "inherited a mess." Donald loves to say he inherited a mess from Obama. But let's stop spraying perfume on this pig: Donald Trump is neither intellectually nor emotionally fit to carry Barack Obama's golf shoes.

The Circus

Wing-It Trump was a hoot last night at his campaign rally. The hog shook off all of John Kelly's Chanel No. 5 and reverted to — Jennifer Rubin's words, not mine — *Crazy Trump*. He undid any good will he might have established at Monday night's Afghanistan address. Wing-It Trump defended his Charlottesville remarks by misquoting his own news conference statements, blaming the media (for reporting his words and actions accurately), and once again propping up his falsely equivalent neo-Nazi-comforting spin.

While speaking in Phoenix — on their political front lawn — Trump bashed Arizona's two GOP senators, one a war hero with brain cancer, even though they could be the only thing standing between him and an early, disgraceful White House exit (let alone getting any legislation done). He proactively annoyed Senate Majority Leader Mitch McConnell (R-Ky.). Apparently Mitch has not done enough to protect the president from the Russian collusion investigation. Wing-It Trump also threatened to shut down the government if Congress doesn't give him his Mexican border wall money.

He did *not* mention murdered anti-Nazi protester Heather Heyer nor the 10 U.S. Navy sailors killed this past week.

Donald performed most of his greatest hits, but even some fans are becoming tired of the rhetorical reruns and childish nicknames: For the first time in Donald Trump's political career, the failing *New York Times,* low-rated *CNN,* and other assorted dishonest fake news outlets reported that people began leaving early. Little Katy Tur (*NBC*), Little George Stephanopoulos (*ABC*), and Little Marco Rubio (GOP senator) had no comment. Otherwise a good time was had by all.

Overall most Americans including many Republicans thought Wing-It Trump's 77-minute circus of a rally last Tuesday was an incompetent, immature, narcissistic mess compared with Monday's (barely) competent, serious, robotic, prompter-matic reading of a speech written by his generals. It was classic Trumpian wing-it vs. teleprompter (ah, let's go for three) *juxtaposition.*

Let's be clear. Donald Trump has created his own presidential mess, the extent of which literally is unprecedented in American history. The only Trump *inheriting* a mess is Barron.■

08/31/17 — Comic Relief: Casual-but-Stylish Disasterwear

[TOPICS: Hurricane Harvey]

In Washington today, White House press secretary Sarah Huckabee Sanders issued a list of the president's movements for the week:

— Monday: Nothing.

— Tuesday: Nothing.

— Wednesday: Good one, some blood.

(— writer's embellishment; thanks to National Lampoon; "Missing White House Tapes"; 1974)

OK, I thought we needed some comic relief this week after devastating floods in Texas, an obscene presidential pardon, more Trump-Russia collusion evidence, and the fear that our country's chief executive might provoke a North Korean nuclear attack. I paraphrased my opening from the classic 1974 National Lampoon comedy album, *Missing White House Tapes* (about Richard Nixon and Watergate). Of course at that time it was *deputy* press secretary *Gerald Warren*. (His boss, press secretary Ron Ziegler, apparently was out to lunch.)

The Dichotomy

The past week has produced tremendous sadness. Houston and other parts of Texas have experienced untold destruction and a still-to-be-determined number of lives lost. As of yesterday, Hurricane (now, Tropical Storm) Harvey has set an all-time record for rainfall in the contiguous United States (50-plus inches over several days), and it's on track to be the most costly U.S. natural disaster.

Deaths are mounting, thousands of people have been rescued, and tens of thousands are displaced, with the numbers — and the water — still rising. As with most American disasters, the spirit of humanity and neighbor helping neighbor has been awesome. Then there was President Trump.

Congratulations Donald, you hit No. 1 — none of these piss-ant, second-rate Obama natural disasters like Hurricanes Irene and Sandy on your watch. Yours is the biggest, the *best*. You are keeping score and you're positively giddy.

The president and first lady visited Texas this week (clearly too soon) ostensibly to survey the damage. Though they didn't go to Houston proper, they still diverted precious resources away from continuing rescue efforts. POTUS and FLOTUS looked like fashion models for the *GQ/Cosmopolitan* line of casual-but-stylish disaster-wear, notwithstanding Melania's caricaturistic high snakeskin stiletto pumps and Hollywood Wayfarers (though it was overcast).

The Donald sported brand new bright brown hiking boots and khakis with nary a scuff or wrinkle to be seen. Mr. Trump, ever concerned with his audience size, addressed a few hundred specta-tors at an impromptu speech in Corpus Christi with, "What a crowd, what a turnout." During his speech and news conference, he did *not* mention the dead, the suffering, the displaced, or the first responders. But he and Melania looked great.

It's distasteful to mix politics with natural disasters. But why stop now? It is stomach-churning to see Donald Trump bring his toxic aura of self-fullness, soul-lessness, and ineptitude to a situation that, though tragic, brings out the best in Americans. Trump and humanity don't go together.

Did I mention his hat? The $40 "USA" Trump-branded cap he modeled at several Hurricane Harvey photo ops that is for sale on his campaign website? An astute member of the fake news press corps suggested sending that $40 to the Red Cross instead.

The Analogy

President Richard Nixon never hawked merchandise at a natural disaster. There has been, however, much discussion about strong parallels between Donald Trump's administration and Nixon's Watergate saga (though it took six *years* for Nixon's troubles to metastasize compared to Trump's six *months*). But more important, consider the parallels between the *Missing White House Tapes* satiric masterpiece and the comic potential of the Trump presidency.

In 1974 there were only three or four TV channels, remote controls were in their infancy, and the internet was just a gleam in ARPANET's eye. This National Lampoon album follows a typical channel surfer manually rotating the mechanical selector, skipping through (parodies of) the popular shows and well-known commercials of the day, with a sardonic Watergate theme applied to each.

In this *day in the life*, the Impeachment Day Parade in progress on Pennsylvania Avenue also is being broadcast. As the viewer turns the knob flipping through channels, she lands on the parade for a minute but gets bored with the early floats: Strangling of the Bald Eagle; Effigy Burning; and Alaska's entry, "A gigantic oil sludge with dead caribou scattered around in it: Quite a personal tribute to Mr. Nixon." The viewer switches over to Big Dick learning how to spell *L-Y-I-N-G* on "Sesame Street." Big Dick also learns to count up to "only" seven: "1-2-3-4-5-6-7." (District Court Judge John Sirica had ordered Nixon to turn over nine secretly recorded Oval Office tapes, but the White House said it had "misspoke," that now "there are only seven.")

Switching to the next channel, the viewer takes in the Lady Plumber "Ring Around the Collar (in this case, *Dollar*)" commercial. (The Plumbers were members of a Nixon White House dirty tricks team commissioned to stop information leaks; they were responsible for the primary Watergate burglaries.) Overly cheery Lady Plumber demonstrates to animated, amazed househusband (National Lampoon actor John Belushi) the benefits of new MexCabbage, which helps to avoid dirty money:

[SING-SONGY KIDS (SUNG TO TUNE OF "RING AROUND THE ROSY"):] "Ring around the dollar. Ring around the dollar."

[HOUSEHUSBAND:] "Holy Maloney! My money's dirty!"

[LADY PLUMBER:] "Sure is. You see, many kinds of improperly laundered funds leave embarrassing telltale traces in bank records and can cause permanent stains on reputations."

[HOUSEHUSBAND:] "No kiddin'?!"

[LADY PLUMBER:] "But Mexican funds, with secret ingredient ITT, keep the White House clean while they prevent the dirt from getting out."

[HOUSEHUSBAND:] "Woooow!"

[LADY PLUMBER:] "All it takes is just a few hundred thousand dollars a month and you can cover up even the worst mess. And thanks to its illegal political action, Mexican money goes to work where it counts, removing all evidence of crimes, greased palms, and dirty tricks in those hard to get at, high places."

[HOUSEHUSBAND:] "Boy, that MexCabbage sure sounds terrific!"

[LADY PLUMBER:] "Use laundered Mexican money — It really pays off!"

> (National Lampoon; *Missing White House Tapes* [LP record album]; 1974.)

Substitute the word *Russian* for *Mexican*, and *VEB* (Russian state bank) for *ITT*, and this skit is as vibrant and relevant as it was in Nixon's day. By the way, another *SNL* alum, Chevy Chase, was a member of National Lampoon and performed on this record.

Also by the way, many of the other *MWHT* skits are just as applicable to the incompetence and corruption of the Trump White House. The short-attention-span television viewer goes on to flip through other parodies of classic commercials and TV shows of the '70s:

— "The Constitution Game" *(which follows the presidential line of succession down to deputy assistant undersecretaries, trying to find an officeholder "clean" enough to assume the presidency)*

— "Mission: Impeachable" *(self-explanatory)*

— Crest commercial *("Daddy! Daddy! I only got three cavities!"* | *"Well, that's swell, Debbie, but I'm in the middle of a press conference."* | *"Mr. Ziegler, uh, The Washington Post reports that your daughter had, in fact, 14 cavities. Care to comment?")*

— Televised Senate Watergate hearings *("What did the president know, and when did he STOP knowing it?")*

— Closing moments of the Impeachment Day Parade, wrapped up by an enthusiastic commentator *("Well that's about it for America's day of shame!")*

— Finally, the Right Reverend Billy Graham performing the swearing-out ceremony *("Goddamn you, Richard Nixon! You son of a b*tch! You lied your a** off! Get the hell out of here! … F*** OFF!")*

(Ibid.; National Lampoon; 1974.)

GOP's Challenge

The swearing-out ceremony of President Donald Trump needs to be expedited. High-level Republicans have started to show some backbone in the past few weeks. A handful of GOP legislators have criticized Trump's disgraceful pardon of convicted (of violating the Constitution) felon, former Arizona Sheriff Joe Arpaio. This was wrong on so many levels — three out of four political pundits (*and* dentists) agree.

National Economic Council Director Gary Cohn told the *Financial Times* that Trump "must do better in consistently and unequivocally" condemning hate groups. Secretary of State Rex Tillerson said that Trump "speaks for himself" when asked about the president's Charlottesville remarks ("very fine people on both sides"). Defense Secretary James Mattis exhorted military members to "hold the line until our country gets back to respecting each other" and can "get the power of inspiration back" (the cause of lost inspirational power obviously being President Trump).

But the U.S. might not be able to hold on until this limited GOP scolding can have an effect. Republican legislators and leaders must "Just say no" to Trump (*and* drugs), *now*. We cannot wait around for Democratic articles of impeachment to crawl through Congress. Republicans — yes, Republicans — must begin calling for the president's resignation in significant numbers. It can happen.

No one thought GOP lawmakers would support Nixon's impeachment — that is until the dam broke after his "Saturday Night Live Massacre" (as Chris Matthews of *MSNBC's Hardball* mistakenly called it in an excited moment). The Saturday Night Massacre occurred when Nixon ordered his attorney general to eliminate the Watergate special prosecutor because the kitchen was getting way too hot. The AG refused. Nixon ultimately had to fire his attorney general *and* his deputy attorney general before he could get to third-in-line Solicitor General Robert Bork who sold his soul and did the deed.

Donald Trump will try to abort the Russia investigation by attempting to eliminate special counsel Robert Mueller. It's inevitable. Trump's White House kitchen already is overcome with heat, smoke, and sparks. I expect Republicans will come around when they finally see the flames. But they shouldn't wait. Senate Majority Leader Mitch McConnell (R-Ky.) has expressed fears that the Trump presidency has caused irreparable damage to the GOP. Scores more whisper about it at cocktail parties and congressional coffee klatches. I implore you, Grand Old Party legislators and leaders, because we need two strong, respectable political parties: Republicans must put up a united front (like the parents of a recalcitrant child) and call for the president's resignation. Now.■

09/07/17 — Trump Administration's Metaphor Offense

[TOPICS: North Korea]

Who's Your Madman?

Have you ever noticed that when political pundits are discussing the North Korean threat and they use the terms *Donald Trump*, *Kim Jong Un*, and *madman* in the same breath, they feel obligated to clarify that the madman in their statement is Kim Jong Un?

> "Of course an unwanted result of our president's narcissistic cluelessness and incessant hot air is that even if Kim Jong Un assumes Trump's threat is an empty one, it still could anger the petulant madman (Kim, that is) to initiate a deadly response."
>
> (Ersin, Tom; "Fire and Fury, and Frankly Power (Ooh, 'FRANKLY' Power!)"; *GraniteWord.com*; 8/10/2017.)

OK, astute readers will note that I cited myself. I know I've heard talking heads make this clarification, too, but I can't find a similar quote from another pundit right now. Having highlighted this issue, I'm counting on my (seven) readers to send me citations for other examples.

But my point stands. Donald Trump is so incompetent, so unhinged in his own right, that pundits and scholars (and pundit-scholars) are compelled to ensure they keep their madmen straight. Because it would be easy to think they were referring to *Trump*, the madman.

Over the past week or two, more statesmen and stateswomen also are in agreement about clarification on this point. *Madman* might be a premature descriptor for President Trump. But *unhinged?* We're there. If you use the terms *Donald Trump, Kim Jong Un,* and *unhinged* in the same breath today, you definitely are obliged to clarify whether the unhinged person to whom you refer is Trump or Kim.

Unhingedly

Donald Trump's latest North Korea tweets alone are unhingedly dangerous:

> "Military solutions are now fully in place, locked and loaded, should North Korea act unwisely. Hopefully Kim Jong Un will find another path!" (8/11/2017.)

> "Kim Jong Un of North Korea made a very wise and well reasoned decision. The alternative would have been both catastrophic and unacceptable!" (8/16/2017.)

Catastrophic *and* unacceptable. In the second tweet, Trump naively implies that his "fire and fury" and "locked and loaded" threats aimed at North Korea earlier in August compelled that country to back down (as ostensibly evidenced by Kim's we'll-wait-and-see response and five days with no new threats). But apparently Kim Jong Un didn't get the memo because only days later he proudly tested a missile-ready hydrogen bomb five or six times stronger than anything he's accomplished to date.

Then President Trump *really* tweeted tough:

> "The United States is considering, in addition to other options, stopping all trade with any country doing business with North Korea [This means you, China]." (9/3/2017.)

"South Korea is finding, as I have told them, that their talk of appeasement with North Korea will not work, they only understand one thing!" (9/3/2017.)

"..North Korea is a rogue nation which has become a great threat and embarrassment to China, which is trying to help but with little success." (9/3/2017.)

"North Korea has conducted a major Nuclear Test. Their words and actions continue to be very hostile and dangerous to the United States....." (9/3/2017.)

President Trump got tough all right: by attacking our ally South Korea (who will bear the brunt of any fire and fury) for "appeasement" and by threatening our trade agreement with them — and by Twitter-shaming China (who we need more than ever), threatening a trade war and criticizing that country's competence. Oh, and Trump scolded Kim again.

World View

Those make up only the tip of the iceberg representing Donald's unhinged communications and actions. But don't just take my word for it:

> *[JAPAN:]* "Trump is escalating the [North Korea] situation by effectively pouring oil on the crisis. A man who is meant to be the leader of the free world but is tweeting random thoughts in the small hours can hardly be considered completely rational. ... He also seems extremely thin-skinned, aggressive, and unwilling to listen to advice, which, to me, makes him quite dangerous."

(Watanabe, Makoto, associate professor of communications and media at Hokkaido Bunkyo University; as cited in Ryall, Julian; "Trump or Kim: Who Are You Calling Crazy? A Dilemma in Japan"; *This Week in Asia*; 8/20/2017.)

[SOUTH KOREA:] "Opinion polls show South Koreans have one of the lowest rates of regard for Trump in the world and they don't consider him to be a reasonable person. In fact, they worry he's kind of nuts, but they still want the alliance."

(Straub, David, Sejong-LS Fellow at The Sejong Institute in South Korea, former head of political section at U.S. embassy in Seoul; as cited in Fifield, Anna; "Seoul Tries to Ignore Trump's Criticism: 'They Worry He's Kind of Nuts,' One Observer Says"; *The Washington Post*; 9/3/2017.)

[GERMANY:] "[A Trump] America that does not care about the rest of the world and just thinks about itself does not make for a big and great country."

(Merkel, Angela, German chancellor; news conference; Berlin, Germany; 8/23/2017.)

[UNITED STATES:] "[President Trump] has not yet been able to demonstrate the stability, nor some of the competence ... to be successful. ... He also recently has not demonstrated that he understands the character of this nation ... [and] what has made this nation great. ... [Without that] our nation is going to go through great peril [unless there is] radical change."

(Corker, Bob, R-Tenn., U.S. Senate Foreign Relations
Committee chair; news conference; Rotary Club of
Chattanooga, Tenn.; 8/17/2017.)

Metaphor Offense

Speaking of lame metaphors and clichés like "didn't get the memo,"
"tip of the iceberg," and "don't just take my word for it," here's the
latest from a Trump administration so-called grownup, U.N. Ambassador Nikki Haley, in response to North Korea's recent successful test of a launchable hydrogen bomb:

> "Enough is enough. The time for half-measures in the Secu-
> rity Council is over. We have kicked the can down the road
> long enough. There is no more road left."

> (Haley, Nikki, R-S.C., U.S. ambassador to U.N., for-
> mer governor; emergency meeting, U.N. Security
> Council; 9/4/2017.)

Now I'm not sure who writes these scripts for Haley. But can't you
just see the president having a hand in it? If he could take time to
write Don Jr.'s press release trying to explain away the Manafort-
Kushner-Don-Jr.-Veselnitskaya Trump Tower Russia-collusion
meeting — especially when Trump Sr. is in no way connected with
Russia, at all, never heard of him, wouldn't recognize the country if
it walked into his office — certainly the president also might want
to put his words into Nikki Haley's mouth for the world stage.

But how effective is this metaphor offense? We know the administration has been honing it for several months as Pyongyang
has increased its testing of bombs and missiles (and President
Trump):

> "What we're going to do is continue to tighten the screws.
> [Kim Jong Un] feels it. He absolutely feels it."

(Haley, Nikki, R-S.C., U.S. ambassador to U.N., former governor; *NBC's Today;* 4/24/2017.)

"[Kim Jong Un] is a pretty smart cookie."

(Trump, Donald, R-N.Y., U.S. president; *CBS News' Face the Nation;* 4/30/2017.) *(reverse metaphorical psychology?)*

"Kim Jong Un is starting to flex his muscles because he feels the pressure. … I think it's a new day when you've got China and the United States working together on a statement to condemn North Korea. They've put pressure on him. He feels it. That's why he's responding this way."

(Haley, Nikki, R-S.C., U.S. ambassador to U.N., former governor; *ABC's This Week* with George Stephanopoulos; 5/14/2017.)

"Spending my 4th [of July] in meetings all day. #ThanksNorthKorea"

(Haley, Nikki, R-S.C., U.S. ambassador to U.N., former governor; Twitter post; 7/4/2017.)

"Done talking about NKorea. China is aware they must act. Japan & SKorea must inc pressure. Not only a US problem. It will req an intl solution."

(Haley, Nikki, R-S.C., U.S. ambassador to U.N., former governor; Twitter post; 7/31/2017.)

"North Korea best not make any more threats to the United
States … [or] they will be met with fire and fury, and frankly
power, the likes of which this world has never seen before."

(Trump, Donald, R-N.Y., U.S. president; news conference; Trump National Golf Club, Bedminster,
N.J.; 8/8/2017.)

And as mentioned, President Trump's "locked and loaded" tweet
came through three days later, Aug. 11.

We're all gonna die.

To be fair, Nikki Haley's "Spending my [July] 4th in meetings
all day" tweet wasn't part of the metaphor offense. She was trying to
avoid calls from Golf Cart One suggesting more offensive metaphors.

[IN OTHER NEWS:] President Trump has rescinded
DACA (Deferred Action for Childhood Arrivals). He said
he "loves" the DREAMers but broke up with them anyway
telling them, "It's not you, it's me."

Call, write, or tweet your legislators to call for Donald Trump's resignation. This is not a metaphor. Pray for peace. Pray for impeachment.

"Remember, Sunday is National Prayer Day (by Presidential
Proclamation)!"

(Trump, Donald, R-N.Y., U.S. president; Twitter
post; 9/2/2017.)

Next week's secret word: *contrived* (as in the contrived presidency
and personality of Donald J. Trump).

Oh, and "Drain the swamp" everyone.■

09/14/17 — Hillary Deserves Her Say

At the 1972 Summer Olympic Games, American Rick DeMont won the gold medal in men's 400-metre freestyle swimming. Brad Cooper took silver. Later when International Olympic Committee members voted to disqualify the top medalist for using performance-enhancing drugs, they didn't give the gold to DeMont's assistant — or his vice president — they gave it to the runner-up, Cooper.

As it should follow with the U.S. presidency. Donald Trump's campaign soon will be found to have cheated in the 2016 election. Once he is impeached and convicted, or resigns, the presidency should not be awarded to his assistant — or vice president. It should go to the runner-up, Hillary Clinton.

Nice try.

What Happened

Simon & Schuster released Hillary's new book, *What Happened*, Tuesday. Numerous previews and sneak peeks have been published and discussed. By now most news and pop culture consumers know that the book outlines Hillary's examination and explanation of her 2016 presidential loss.

One of the surrounding subplots is the reporting that many Democrats, including in leadership, rue the book's release and subsequent book tour because they believe the party needs to move on. They view it as a negative distraction heading into the next election season. They don't want multiple news cycles dedicated to excuses and sour grapes running into 2018.

But really. What could she do? What would anyone else in her sensible flats do? Almost no one in Hillary Clinton's position, having gone through what she has gone through, couldn't *not* tell her story. (Ooh, a triple negative.) And she did get it out as soon as possible to minimize any negative 2018 effects. The woman has been wronged for 25 years as the target of herculean disinformation campaigns and ridiculous but persistent conspiracy theories. I am sick of constantly hearing the qualifier that *she* must accept blame for her 2016 loss, too. No one runs a perfect campaign. Of course she must accept *some* blame.

But so must all close *winners*, if they were to have lost. Al Franken is a political genius because he beat Minnesota's 2008 GOP incumbent senator, Norm Coleman, by 312 votes, or 41.99% to 41.98%. If that had been flipped, you don't think Al would have soul-searched that result to death? You don't think he would have blamed the Coleman campaign's DeHumorizer™ (trademarked by Al), which presented many of Al's old jokes and humorous writings literally, without the Franken irony, and displayed them out of context for maximum damage? And like Hillary, Mr. Franken being an author, you don't think he would have been compelled to respond to fair-weather fans criticizing him because he couldn't pull out a measly 312 more votes, thereby costing Dems a filibuster-proof Senate?

Unlike most other election losers (here it comes), Hillary *won more votes* — about 2.86 million more. Have you heard about that!? A change of only 77,000 or so votes (about 0.6%) in the Midwest would have given her the College — 77,000 votes out of 13 million cast in three key states. And you can multiply that unfair DeHumorizer™ handicap by a hundred.

A presidential campaign is extremely complicated, and those in leadership make strategy decisions based on what they know at the time. I'm fed up with hearing she should have gone to Michigan, Wisconsin, and Pennsylvania. Now that we know Russia was helping Donald, and after FBI Director James Comey's misguided reopening of email-gate at the eleventh hour, a hundred trips to the Blue Wall might not have made a difference.

Reasonable Person

In legislative and legal theory there exists a concept called the *reasonable person:*

> "[A reasonable person is] someone who uses such qualities as attention, knowledge, intelligence, and judgment which a society requires of its members to protect their own interests and the interests of others."

> (Gifis, Steven H.; "Reasonable Person"; *Barron's Law Dictionary;* 2016.)

> "The reasonable person knows that ice is slippery, that live wires are dangerous, that alcohol impairs driving ability, and that children might run into the street when they are playing."

> ("Negligence"; legal dictionary in *TheFreeDictionary.com;* 2017.)

Donald Trump said repeatedly during the campaign that Hillary "doesn't have the stamina" and "she just doesn't look presidential." The reasonable person knows this was his way of reminding us constantly that his opponent was a woman, the same way he reminded everyone regularly in 2012 that Barack Obama is Black (and probably born in Kenya). And for those sexist or closet-sexist men (and some women), Trump's dog-whistled digs at Hillary's gender tugged at their bias. Trump told us — through these and a thousand other examples — who he is. A reasonable person knows Donald Trump is a sexist who's not afraid to use his sexism and to fight dirty in other ways.

The Trump campaign and administration has sought to hide all their many contacts with Russia. They mendaciously denied their numerous meetings with Russian emissaries. When discovered, the administration repeatedly told more lies to explain those meetings away. When the FBI investigation was getting warmer, President Trump fired the director to stop "this Russia thing." A reasonable person knows that for some reason Donald Trump is trying desperately to hide all-things Russia from the American people.

More of "This Russia Thing"

With or without the Trump campaign's help, we now know that Russian-backed actors disseminated and promoted a tremendous amount of Hillary Clinton disinformation. We'll never know how many votes were swung. But a reasonable person knows it was a significant number.

With or without the Trump campaign's help, we now know that Russian-backed actors hacked Democratic National Committee and Clinton campaign staff email accounts and leaked unimportant but embarrassing internal communications — the types of communications any political campaign has and would want kept private. The funny thing is they also hacked the Republican National Committee but only leaked *Democratic* emails. A reasonable person deduces this effort was coordinated to help the Trump campaign.

Eleven days before Election Day, Hillary was up by double digits in the polls, then FBI Director James Comey wrongly reopened her email server investigation. By Election Day eve, though vindicated, she was down to a lead of low single digits. A reasonable person can see the late-campaign Comey actions cost Clinton a significant amount of votes.

Brad Cooper ultimately got the Olympic gold medal he deserved. Now it's almost time to give Hillary the presidency. A reasonable person can see that if you eliminate the cheating and FBI mistakes, she won. After eight months of Trump in office, we know that competence, intelligence, maturity, experience, and integrity count for something. And Donald has realized he can't build a successful administration on a steady diet of narcissistic prevarication and reality-show shenanigans. Did I mention he's dangerously in-competent?

OK, the presidency is not a gold medal. When Donald Trump ultimately is forced out of office due to obstruction of justice, collusion with Russia, financial corruption, criminal nepotism, felonious narcissism, or plain old incompetence (25th Amendment?), Vice President Mike Pence will be our president. If Pence is too tied to the Trump mess, House Speaker Paul Ryan will be the guy. Either one will be a poor choice but still miles above President Trump.

Let's expedite the inevitable. Contact your legislators and tell them a reasonable person would be calling for President Trump's resignation. ∎

09/21/17 — Please, Please, Mr. President, Don't Call Me Rocket Man

[TOPICS: North Korea]

"You're showing the world that you're so easy with an insult … about our leader."

(Conway, Kellyanne, counselor to the president [Trump]; *Fox News' Fox & Friends;* 9/18/2017.)

Yes, Kellyanne Conway experienced an *A Christmas Carol*-style transformation. She had a midnight visit from the ghost of former "business partner" Paul Manafort, still trapped in his ethereal chains of greed and presidential campaign treachery. After Paul left, the Ghosts of Presidents Past, Present, and Yet to Come took her on a psychic journey of self-reflection and contrition. The next morning she went on *Fox & Friends* and pointedly criticized her boss, Donald Trump, for his five-year campaign of promoting knowingly false conspiracy theories, ignorant commentary, and yes, numerous insults directed at "our leader," President Barack Obama.

Kellyanne Stands Up for the Boss

All seriousness aside, Kellyanne did say these words; however, they were in criticism of the previous night's *69th Primetime Emmy Awards*, which leaned heavily on jokes at President Trump's expense. But can you *believe* the blatant hypocrisy of Kellyanne Conway!? "Easy With an Insult" could be Donald Trump's nickname, and one of the *kinder* ones. Insults are what he does. Insults are his trademark. And his base of in-and-out-of-the-racist-closet, support-Trump-no-matter-what-because-he-hates-PC-like-I-do hyper tribalists love it.

Of course the other 60% of Americans and probably 90% of world citizens are embarrassed (and frightened) by Trump's antics. But we have this tedious set of regulations (the Constitution) that says if the guy got himself elected president, no matter by what fantastical perfect Stormy (or storm), we've got to put up with him until he is impeached and convicted or resigns to avoid that outcome.

Kellyanne's comments on *Fox & Friends* were particularly hypocritical in light of President Trump's debut at the annual United Nations General Assembly fall meetings this week. Try to imagine what is going through the heads of world leaders and high-level foreign diplomats as they meet and shake hands with ol' Easy With an Insult Donald on opening day, Monday. Then put yourself in their heads as they listen to our president's first foreign policy speech to the world Tuesday.

GraniteWord.com has obtained exclusive access to diary entries made this week by foreign leaders and diplomats chronicling their interactions with President Trump and their reactions to his speech (— *writer's embellishment*).

Monday: Meet-and-Greet Over Complementary Continental Breakfast

[U.N. SECRETARY-GENERAL ANTONIO GUTERRES:] Dear Diary, At the U.N. breakfast, I spotted President Trump across the room and he approached. Donald offered me his signature overdone handshake and said he wants to "make the United Nations great," but he left off the *again* part — his way of saying it never was great I guess. My mind wandered to his characterization of American conservative columnist Charles Krauthammer, who is paralyzed from the waist down, as "a guy that can't buy a pair of pants."

> (as Charles Krauthammer indeed was characterized by Trump, Donald, R-N.Y., presidential primary candidate; interview conducted by Roberts, Thomas; *MSNBC*; 7/18/2015.)

[BRITISH FOREIGN SECRETARY BORIS JOHNSON:] Dear Diary, At the meet-and-greet I saw an orange flash from the corner of my eye, the only haircut in the room worse than mine. President Trump was armed with a recent quote from Phil Hogan, Britain's Agriculture Commissioner. Donald shook my hand and said, "What's this I hear about, 'Mr. Johnson … behaving and acting and speaking strangely … his reputation is not good and he is a diminished figure in the government'?" I cleverly responded, "Yes, Mr. President. Welcome to *your* world, eh?" I immediately thought of my beloved Marina as I recalled a Trump tweet directed at one of his former competitors: "Be careful, Lyin' Ted, or I will spill the beans on your wife!"

> (as indeed tweeted publicly to Sen. Ted Cruz by Trump, Donald, R-N.Y., presidential primary candidate; Twitter post; 3/23/2016.)

Tuesday: President Trump's First Speech to the United Nations General Assembly

[GERMAN CHANCELLOR ANGELA MERKEL:] Dear Diary, Though I couldn't make it to New York, I'm watching a recording of President Trump's UNGA address. When will he learn how to use a teleprompter? He's saying something about "we will have no choice but to totally destroy North Korea" and calling Kim Jong Un "Rocket Man." Sure, Donald is using middle school putdowns to threaten nuclear war on 25 or 35 million people, but all I can think of are his comments at a rally about Hillary returning a few seconds late from a debate bathroom break: "I know where she went — it's disgusting, I don't want to talk about it *(Donald titters; audience chuckles)*. No, it's too disgusting. Don't say it; it's disgusting *(Donald smiles bigly; audience roars with laughter)*."

(as Hillary Clinton indeed was joked about by Trump, Donald, R-N.Y., presidential primary candidate; campaign rally;
Grand Rapids, Mich.; 12/21/2015.)

[PAKISTAN PRIME MINISTER SHAHID KHAQAN ABBASI:]
Dear Diary, Today President Trump wrestled the U.N. teleprompter
and lost. He referred to "loser terrorists," which filled my mind with
"Little Marco," "Lyin' Ted," "Crooked Hillary," "Low-Energy Jeb,"
"Little Katy," and so many others. Is that all he's got? I do like his
father-daughter relationship with Ivanka though. He speaks very
highly of her: "Yeah, she's really something, and what a beauty, that
one. If I weren't happily married and, ya know, her *father* ..."

> (as adult daughter Ivanka Trump indeed was fantasized
> about by Trump, Donald, R-N.Y., presidential primary can-
> didate; interview conducted by Solotaroff, Paul; *Rolling Stone;*
> 7/18/2015.)

[MYANMAR STATE COUNSELOR AUNG SAN SUU KYI:]
Dear Diary, And I think *my* country has image problems. At least I
can read a teleprompter without doing the robot. I'm home watching President Trump tell the U.N. General Assembly that the world
faces "great peril." But what about American women? All I can
think of when I see this man is Donald talking about Megyn Kelly's
"blood coming out of her — wherever." All because Megyn pointed
out that he calls women he doesn't like "fat pigs, dogs, slobs, and
disgusting animals," which he laughed off by replying, "only Rosie
O'Donnell."

> (comments about Megyn Kelly, Rosie O'Donnell, other
> women, as indeed admitted to by Trump, Donald, R-N.Y.,
> presidential primary candidate; during, after Republican pres-
> idential primary debate; 8/6/2015.)

[IRANIAN PRESIDENT HASSAN ROUHANI:] Dear Diary, This afternoon I tried listening to the American president dis us by accusing Iran of being "out of compliance" with the nuclear deal. But all I could think about was that poor Carly Fiorina, when Trump said during an interview upon seeing his only female primary rival appear on the TV, "Look at that face! Would anyone vote for that? ... Really, folks, come on. Are we *serious?*" Even the Ayatollah thinks Donald has a low opinion of women.

> (as Carly Fiorina indeed was characterized by Trump, Donald, R-N.Y., presidential primary candidate; interview conducted by Solotaroff, Paul; *Rolling Stone;* 7/18/2015.)

Dead Horses

I think my point is clear, but let me beat a dead horse into the ground another time or two. Donald Trump is "easy with an insult." This applies to the locker room as well as the world stage. He has no filter and no moral compass. When you add his adolescent insults to his large number of incredibly stupid policy statements, bankruptcies, and dishonest dealings, you have to wonder how the guy gets through life.

If he hadn't inherited Daddy's property empire and several hundred million dollars, Mr. Trump barely would be able to hold together a local RE/MAX real estate office. There would be no *The Apprentice*, no *Celebrity Apprentice*, no Trump Tower, no Trump International Golf Courses, no Trump Water, no Trump Steaks, no Trump University — and no Ivanka because Ivana never would have given The Donald a second look. On the upside, no Don Jr.

Do we really believe world leaders don't think about the blusterous Trump inanities when they're shaking his hand — or worse, his past empty threats when they're across the negotiating table from him? They can't *not* think about these things. Is it not obvious they must be asking themselves, Why would this guy be straight with me when he's double-crossed so many others including his own political party? Are they not reminding themselves that the name *Trump* is synonymous with *lie?* And are they not wondering how much longer special prosecutor Robert Mueller will let this guy be president?

Most frightening of all, are they not fearful of what insulting nickname President Trump will bestow upon them? I mean c'mon. If I'm Kim Jong Un, I could take my country being bombed off the map with "fire and fury, the likes of which the world has never seen." But please, please, Mr. President, don't call me Rocket Man.◾

09/28/17 — Nobody Knew That Obamacare Repeal and Replace Could Be so Complicated

"It's an unbelievably complex subject. Nobody knew that health care could be so complicated."

(Trump, Donald, R-N.Y., U.S. president; meeting with governors; White House; 2/27/2017.)

This week Senate Republicans canceled the scheduled vote on their latest attempt to repeal the Affordable Care Act. The Graham-Cassidy bill had been on shaky ground for several days. After Sen. Susan Collins (R-Maine) joined Rand Paul (R-Ky.) and John McCain (R-Ariz.) by announcing her "no" vote Monday, Graham, Cassidy, and Leader McConnell folded their hand. The bill could afford to lose no more than two Republicans or it was dead (all 48 Democratic caucus members had committed to vote "no"). Speculation has it there also were two or three *undeclared* Republican "no" votes.

This third (or fourth?) failure since President Trump's inauguration was significant because it was the Senate GOP majority's (52-48) last chance to pass an Obamacare repeal by only 50 votes or more (50 plus VP Mike Pence's tie-breaker) instead of a filibuster-proof 60 votes or more. A deadline materialized due to the Senate parliamentarian's recent determination that after Sept. 30, 2017, the bill could be filibustered by Democrats.

This leaves me with two questions: 1) Why this surprise, seemingly arbitrary cutoff date (apparently related to budget reconciliation and the fiscal year)? and 2) Why didn't the Senate parliamentarian get her 15 minutes of fame?

Bigger Question

But the far bigger question is: Why couldn't the Republicans get it done? As everyone not on life support knows, GOP leaders and legislators have been promising America an Obamacare repeal since it was passed in 2010. They ran, raised large amounts of money, and were elected on this promise. During the time they had the House and Senate but not the White House, they made a show of sending dozens of bills to weaken or repeal O'care to President Obama's desk knowing he would never sign them. But since they finally got the White House, too, in January 2017, they've tried and failed multiple times to get an ACA-kill bill to President Trump. Why did they fail?

It's simple: The American people as a whole no longer believe the many lies they were told about the Affordable Care Act during and after its passage.

Young Democratic voters, you think they lied about *Hillary*!? The mendacity surrounding Obamacare was just as vicious and pernicious — because they hated Barack Obama even more than Hillary Clinton, believe it or not.

President Obama Is Human

There were so many falsehoods and misconceptions flying (I call this *prevaricatum verbosium:* an avalanche of lies, too many for listeners to remember), it was extremely difficult for fact-checkers to keep up the debunking — very similar to today's era of Trump. (OK. It's hard to believe but the Trump era is worse.)

Let's get this out of the way first:

> "If you like your health care plan, you keep your health care plan."

> (Obama, Barack, D-Ill, U.S. president; town hall
> meeting; Central High School, Grand Junction, Colo.
> [and many other instances]; 8/15/2009.)

Republicans have touted this as the greatest lie since Bill Clinton averred, "I did not have sexual relations with that woman." But Obama was not lying. At worst he made a mistake. Furthermore he only was half-wrong. His mistake was not accounting for the normal "churn rate" of employees and policyholders who switch jobs and insurance companies. A new job certainly could bring a new insurer who is obligated to meet the new (better) ACA minimum standards of coverage and has different eligible providers.

President Obama was half-right in that so-called grandfathered plans, in existence before March 23, 2010, did not have to meet all the new coverage requirements. Those insurers' existing policyholders did not have to change anything — until and unless the insurer made significant changes to their plans or the employee changed jobs. Additionally policies on the ACA health care exchanges were *new* (not grandfathered) plans, so if you switched to one of those, coverage and providers certainly could change.

Barack Obama ultimately acknowledged that his promise went too far. In a Nov. 7, 2013, *NBC News* interview with Chuck Todd, he offered the following apology: "I am sorry that [many Americans] are finding themselves in this situation based on assurances they got from me. We've got to work hard to make sure that they know we hear them and that we're going to do everything we can to deal with folks who find themselves in a tough position as a consequence of this."

Prevaricatum Verbosium (Numerous Lies)

Now that we've cleared that up, let's reminisce about the following intentional lies from anti-Obamacare fabulists:

Death Panels: "The sick, the elderly, and the disabled … will have to stand in front of Obama's 'death panel' so his bureaucrats can decide, based on a subjective judgment of their 'level of productivity in society,' whether they are worthy of health care."

(Palin, Sarah, R-Alaska, former governor, 2008 [John McCain] vice presidential candidate; Facebook post [and many other instances]; 8/7/2009.)

Forced Benefit Options, Free Health Care for Undocumented: "Page 42: The 'Health Choices Commissioner' will decide health benefits for you. You will have no choice. … Page 50: All non-U.S. citizens, illegal or not, will be provided with free health care services."

(chain email; 7/28/2009; as cited in Holan, Angie Drobnic; "No Free Health Care for Illegal Immigrants in the Health Bill"; *PolitiFact;* 7/30/2009.)

Government Takeover: "This is a government takeover of our health care system. It is the government basically running the entire health care system."

(Ryan, Paul, R-Wis., U.S. representative; "Politico Interview: Rep. Paul Ryan"; *Politico* [and many other instances]; 3/23/2010.)

IRS Database: "Your health care, my health care, all the Fox viewers' health care, their personal, intimate, most close-to-the-vest secrets will be in that database, and the IRS is in charge of that database?"

(Bachmann, Michele, R-Minn., U.S. representative, 2012 presidential primary candidate; *Fox News' On the Record* with Greta Van Susteren; 5/15/2013.)

Job Losses: "75% of small businesses now say they are going to be forced to either fire workers or cut their hours."

(Rubio, Marco, R-Fla., U.S. senator; "America, It's Not too Late to Stop Obamacare"; *FoxNews.com* [and many other instances]; 7/25/2013.)

Muslims Exempt: "Obamacare … on page 107 … allows the establishment of Dhimmitude and Sharia Muslim diktat in the United States. Muslims are specifically exempted from the government mandate to purchase insurance, and also from the penalty tax for being uninsured."

(chain email; 5/29/2013; as cited in Holan, Angie Drobnic; "Have You Ever Heard of 'Dhimmitude'?"; *PolitiFact*; 5/30/2013.)

Rationing, Tax Increases, Job Losses: "Obamacare will result in the rationing of health care, significant tax increases, [and] significant job losses."

(Scott, Rick, R-Fla., governor; statement to reporter; as cited in *Sunshine State News* [and many other instances]; 8/11/2011.)

Tax Increases: "Obamacare is … the largest tax increase in the history of the world."

(Limbaugh, Rush; *The Rush Limbaugh Show*; 6/28/2012.)

Had enough? All of these have been disproved thoroughly, many without much effort. And I didn't even document at least this many *other* widespread myths and false predictions such as the following: people over age 76 are not eligible for cancer treatment; Americans won't enroll, and if they do they won't pay their premiums; there is a 3.8% sales tax on all real estate transactions; it will kill the economy; sporting goods are taxed as medical devices; it won't reduce the uninsured rate; it's a government takeover of one-sixth of the economy; your sex life will be questioned; it will lead to higher deficits; the government will allow forced home inspections; it was rammed through Congress in a hurry, with no GOP participation; Obamacare is socialism; etc.

Many anti-Obama zealots on many right-wing media platforms repeated these myths, lies, and misconceptions incessantly. Consequently, legitimate media outlets felt obligated to report on the misconceptions, giving them even more attention.

Again, Why Did Obamacare Repeal Fail?

In the first couple of years after Congress passed the ACA, two factors supported the repeal effort: 1) too many Americans still believed the fallacious propaganda; and 2) not enough people had seen the benefits of the bill. Unfortunately the repeated, repetitious, and redundant repeating of lies works: Large numbers of people begin believing them despite logical, factual refutations. Doubly unfortunately, Republicans as a whole have no compunction about taking advantage of that fact. This was how W. and VP Dick Cheney got us into the Iraq War: relentlessly repeating (falsely), "WMDs! Weapons of Mass Destruction! WMDs!" (as in, Iraq had 'em, though they didn't). This was how they disguised torture as "enhanced interrogation techniques." This was how Donald defeated presidential candidate Hillary Clinton. And this was how a Trump Congress *almost* defeated, then *almost* repealed, the Affordable Care Act.

In the early days the battle cry simply was "Repeal." There was nothing to *replace* because, as noted, not enough people had experienced any real benefits yet. After a few years, however, Republicans were forced to adjust their slogan to "Repeal *and Replace*." More and more Americans began realizing the GOP had lied to them and that the ACA helped many people.

As the 2016 presidential campaign unfolded, millions of Americans were benefiting from Obamacare, and Republicans had to keep sweetening the Repeal and Replace deal. Then Donald Trump came along and made intentionally false promises that caused GOP leaders' heads to explode:

> "We're going to have insurance for everybody. There was a philosophy in some circles that if you can't pay for it, you don't get it. That's not going to happen with us. [People covered under Obamacare] can expect to have great health care. It will be in a much-simplified form. Much less expensive, and much better."
>
> (Trump, Donald, R-N.Y., U.S. president-elect; as cited in Costa, Robert & Goldstein, Amy; "Trump Vows 'Insurance for Everybody' in Obamacare Replacement Plan"; *The Washington Post* [and many other instances]; 1/15/2017.)

Got that? Trump says everyone covered. Much better health care. Less expensive health care. Simpler heath care.

Here's Why

This is why Repeal and Replace has failed: Because the only way the GOP could have kept even its minimal commitments was with a health care system that looked a lot like Obamacare. And no matter how much Mitch McConnell, Donald Trump, Paul Ryan, et al. lied to us by saying their last three or four health care bills fulfilled anything near those commitments, the American people finally saw through it. When citizens were threatened with losing the health care they finally had secured, they organized, they protested, and they swayed the moral sensibilities of enough Republican senators to do the right thing. Now Republicans are compelled to work with Democrats to fix the ACA (as President Obama and Democrats always have promoted) instead of killing it.

Back in the late 1980s and early '90s, Apple sued Microsoft for stealing the concept of "windows" for computer operating systems. (Apple sued even though *it* stole the idea — and the idea for the "mouse" — from Xerox PARC in 1979.) *Windows* was a layperson's term for "graphical user interface" or GUI. It was a complicated settlement, but Microsoft essentially won based upon the judge's (and his technical advisers') opinion that *any* GUI would have to look like some form of graphic *windows* opening and closing.

And so it is with health care. If you want to maximize the number of Americans with affordable health care coverage — without going to a single-payer system — it hinges on three things: 1) individual mandate (everyone must buy in); 2) subsidies for those who can't afford full price; and 3) elimination of preexisting condition preclusions. In other words it must look a lot like the Affordable Care Act. The people finally learned this in spite of the lies. And at least three GOP senators learned this.

Nobody knew that repealing and replacing Obamacare could be so complicated.■

10/05/17 — That Whole "Unable to Discharge the Duties of President" Thing, and Sen. Bob Corker

If Donald Trump were a job applicant for any position outside of his own family business, he likely could not get hired. If he did sneak by some unwitting HR manager, he would be canned long before his probationary period was up. Trump is a unique combination of incompetence and immorality. Yet just the right combination of Americans (though not a majority) voted to hire him as president.

What Were They Thinking?

The question, "What were they thinking?" has been asked and examined in every possible light. This quandary will be debated for decades if not centuries. In office less than nine months, I suspect President Trump has secured the top spot on most presidential historians' lists of all-time worst U.S. chief executives (though Doris Kearns Goodwin, Jon Meacham, and Michael Beschloss probably won't confirm this until after his ouster). The Donald has failed every test for presidential competency and ethical behavior.

These failures fall into three primary categories: 1) financial corruption and use of the presidency to enrich himself; 2) likely illegal collusion with the Russian government to get elected; and 3) obstruction of justice, i.e., blocking the investigation into that likely Russian collusion.

A second tier of categories — evidencing not illegal though dangerously immoral reasons for President Trump's unfitness for office — comprises blatant racism and sexism, ubiquitous mendacity, colossal dearth of empathy, governance by narcissism (whatever makes him look good), governance by vindictiveness (whatever makes former President Obama look bad), governance by distraction (e.g., threatening war to distract from his failures and bad press), and sheer lack of intelligence and critical thinking, i.e., incompetence.

What Have We Learned?

We've learned that Republican politicians with integrity make up a very small minority of the party. The majority of elected GOP officials have been presented with a plethora (good word) of reasons to abandon their support for the president. Nonetheless they stick with him, apparently from fear of being "primary-ed" (losing their next GOP primary to a more-pro-Trumper) — and also to get their tax cuts, for themselves and their wealthy donors.

There are, however, a number of reasonable, ethical Republican thinkers who are concerned about the future of their party and more importantly the country. Jennifer Rubin, Charlie Sykes, Bill Kristol, George Will, Nicolle Wallace, Steve Schmidt, Richard Painter, Ana Navarro, Max Boot, Rick Wilson, Mark Salter, David Frum, and others continue to tell the sad truth about the man who has kidnapped their party. Keep it up, my friends.

But it is the rare Republican truth-teller who occupies a seat in Congress. One of those is highly respected Senate Foreign Relations Committee Chair Bob Corker of Tennessee, though even Sen. Corker comes with a caveat. To paraphrase Nicolle Wallace, former (George W. Bush) White House communications director, on her cable news show this past week, the senator has swallowed the truth serum of retirement. He announced last month that he will not seek reelection in November 2018. No matter.

What Has GOP Sen. Bob Corker Learned?

Sen. Corker has been one of the miniscule number of GOP congresspersons to say aloud what so many must be thinking. And the beautiful thing is he has over a year left to call out Trump from his Republican Senate seat pulpit.

"[The White House is] in a downward spiral right now and [has] got to figure out a way to come to grips with all that's happening. You know the shame of it is there's a really good national security team in place … But the chaos that is being created by the lack of discipline is creating … a worrisome environment."

(Corker, Bob, R-Tenn., U.S. Senate Foreign Relations Committee chair; statement to reporters; outside U.S. Senate chamber; 5/15/2017.)

"The president has not yet been able to demonstrate the stability nor some of the competence that he needs to demonstrate in order to be successful. He has not demonstrated that he understands what has made this nation great and what it is today, and he's got to demonstrate the characteristics of a president who understands that."

(Corker, Bob, R-Tenn., U.S. Senate Foreign Relations Committee chair; statement to reporters; Rotary Club meeting, Chattanooga, Tenn.; *Nooga.com;* 8/17/2017.)

"Sen. Bob Corker suggested Wednesday that Gens. John Kelly and James Mattis, as well as Secretary of State Rex Tillerson are the 'people that help separate our country from chaos,' a stinging criticism of President Donald Trump from a man once considered an ally in Washington. Asked directly by a reporter whether he was referring to Trump in using the word 'chaos,' Corker … responded: '[Mattis, Kelly, and Tillerson] work very well together to make sure the policies we put forth around the world are sound and coherent. There are other people within the adminstration that don't. I hope they stay because they're valuable to the national security of our nation.' … Reread that last paragraph. The sitting Republican chairman of the Senate Foreign Relations Committee is suggesting that if Tillerson was removed from office (or quit), the national security of the country would potentially be in danger. And he's refusing to knock down — and thereby affirming — the idea that Trump is an agent of chaos who pushes policies that are not always 'sound' or 'coherent.' That. Is. Stunning."

> (Cillizza, Chris; "Bob Corker Just Told the World What He Really Thinks of Donald Trump"; *CNN.com*; 10/5/2017.)

That Whole *"President Is Unable to Discharge the Powers and Duties of His Office"* Thing

What else have we learned? That the Founding Fathers and 20th century legislators did not adequately think through that whole "President is unable to discharge the powers and duties of his office" thing.

There's been a lot of talk about the 25th Amendment to the Constitution, especially the first paragraph of the last section *(Section 4)*:

> *"Whenever the Vice President and a majority of either the principal officers of the executive departments* or of such other body as Congress may by law provide, transmit to the President pro tempore of the Senate and the Speaker of the House of Representatives *their written declaration that the President is unable to discharge the powers and duties of his office*, the Vice President shall immediately assume the powers and duties of the office as Acting President." *(— italics added)*

This means that Vice President Mike Pence and a majority of the other Trump sycophants in his Cabinet must get together and decide that Donald J. Trump is unfit for office even though he's not in a persistent vegetative state or suffering from screaming psychotic episodes (my apologies to psychotics). The amendment goes on to say that if the president disagrees (i.e., thinks he *is* still fit for the job), then two-thirds of both houses of Congress must agree to remove him from office.

President Trump could prompt a nuclear war, start a civil war, drain the treasury (not the swamp), or cause another Great Depression before that will ever happen.

What the founders and later Congress failed to plan for was the possibility of a Trumpian phenomenon in which a professional grifter could fool enough of the people enough of the time to get elected. He benefited from a perfect electoral storm of quirks and coincidences, along with massive foreign (and domestic) propaganda. He took over a major political party and is holding that party's psyche hostage. He's brainwashed a powerful minority of the electorate. And he is a very bad man.

The 25th ½ Amendment: Presidential Probationary Period

The 25th Amendment needs a *Section 5* that deals with a probationary period for the presidency just like any other job in America. McDonald's wouldn't keep a burger flipper on the grill line after 30 days of exhibiting the characteristics that Donald has. A waitstaff member at Trump Tower would have been let go within weeks of behaving as our president has. And I'm sorry to disparage burger flippers and waitstaff with the comparison.

Section 5 would put the new president on probation by the American people. The standard probationary period in U.S. employment culture is 90 days. OK, we'll double that for POTUS. A confirmatory election could be held the first Tuesday after the first Monday in the July after each new president is inaugurated the first time. The voters who realized they were snowed by Donald Trump would have a face-saving way to correct their mistake. The Republicans who always vote GOP no matter what would have a second chance to realize there could be something worse than a Democrat in the Oval Office.

Oh, and if the president doesn't make it through probation, the runner-up candidate gets the job.

All seriousness aside, the only option we have left is to promote a loud demand for President Trump's resignation. If the (Senate Republican) Bob Corkers, Jeff Flakes, and John McCains in Washington would go a little further, we could hope for a call to step down, so deafening the president would be forced to heed it. Even Richard Nixon came to a point when a large enough loss of support prompted him do the right thing if only to save face.

It's never happened, you say? The country also has never seen the most vile, egomaniacal confidence artist ever to befoul a television screen make it to the White House.■

10/12/17 — National Review: "Between the Hysterical and the Lunatic," and More Sen. Bob Corker

I recently read Matthew Continetti's Oct. 7, 2017, article:

"Pop Goes the Liberal Media Bubble: Trump Drives the Mainstream Press to Abandon the Pretense of Objectivity"

It appeared first in the *Washington Free Beacon* (of which Continetti is editor in chief), then the *National Review*, both respected conservative publications. Indeed, my firebrand ninth grade social studies and government teacher, Gerald Eggen, taught us that the *National Review* was the prominent conservative magazine in America, *The New Republic* was the preeminent liberal voice, and we students needed to know the difference. (Sadly in the 21st century, the latter seems to have fallen from grace among many liberal thinkers.)

Mainstream Media: "Somewhere Between the Hysterical and the Lunatic"

The title of Continetti's article tells the reader everything about the author's perspective. Early in the piece, he continues to establish his bias ("and that's, *OK*" — *thanks to SNL's Stuart Smalley, aka Al Franken*):

> "The overall tone of coverage of this president and his administration is somewhere between the hysterical and the lunatic. ... The mode of knee-jerk disgust ... prevents the mainstream media from distinguishing between the genuinely interesting stories and the false, partisan, and hackwork ones."

> (Continetti, Matthew; "Pop Goes the Liberal Media
> Bubble: Trump Drives the Mainstream Press to
> Abandon the Pretense of Objectivity"; *Washington
> Free Beacon, National Review;* 10/7/2017.)

First, there always is a problem when conservatives refer to the "mainstream press" or "mainstream media." The labels are so wide as to include many outlets' journalism practices that do *not* apply to, say, *The Washington Post* and *The New York Times.* Pundits like Continetti create great leeway for themselves by criticizing the mainstream media without defining it. As I address some of his points, I will define it as *The Washington Post* and *The New York Times* (or *Post/Times* for short), at least concerning print media. (If he's talking television, I'll include *ABC News, NBC News, CBS News, CNN,* and *MSNBC.* Since he often appears on the "liberal" *MSNBC,* Matthew must begrudge it *some* credibility.)

Second, inherent in Mr. Continetti's article title and content is the canard of the mainstream media being synonymous with "the liberal press." Ask Bill and Hillary Clinton if the *Post/Times* went easy on them during their campaign trials and tribulations and during many stretches of Bill's presidency. It's because of the mainstream media that references such as *the blue dress, Hillary's emails, the meaning of* is, *Benghazi,* and so many more now are ingrained in our collective cultural consciousness.

A) Use of False Equivalency

Third, Matthew Continetti's premise begs for a discussion of false equivalency. This term has been thrown around (and maligned) a lot in the past decade. My definitive examples follow: A) There is the use of it (commonly by Republicans); and B) There is the attempted foisting of it upon journalists and news outlets in the name of neutrality.

"An illustration of false equivalency was when many conservatives tried to equate these two things: 1) Senate Majority Leader Harry Reid (D-Nev.) using the term *Negro* (without any irony) to designate African Americans in a private conversation; and 2) former Senate Majority Leader Trent Lott (R-Miss.) opining, at former Sen. Strom Thurmond's (R-S.C.) open-to-reporters 100th birthday party, that America would be better off if Thurmond (and his platform of institutional segregation) had won the 1948 presidential election.

"OK, Reader. You just heard the comparison of one faux pas to another. Do you say to yourself, 'Yeah, Reid was just as guilty as Lott was and Reid also should resign'? Or do you take an extra few seconds to actively listen to what you just heard? You might then say to yourself, 'Wait a minute. Harry Reid — who played a key role in drafting the first Black U.S. president to run for the office — used an outdated though proper-for-its-time ethnic term, an innocent mistake for an old white guy. Reid exhibited no real bigotry. But Lott joked, the way a joke indicates one's true beliefs, that a President Strom Thurmond (ergo legal segregation) would have been better for our country. Now that's real racism and Lott appropriately was forced to resign.'

"If you said these two examples are *not* equivalent, you just reasoned in a critically thoughtful manner."

(Ersin, Tom; "False Equivalency Meets Active Listening"; *Barack vs. the Anti-PC: Laying the Groundwork for a 2016 Donald Trump Presidential Run;* 2017.)

In his article, Continetti can't stop himself from invoking one of Donald Trump's favorite canards (sorry, I really needed that word again). He accuses highly respected economist Paul Krugman of circulating "fake news" — about cholera breaking out in Puerto Ri-

co — in support of an effort to make the incompetent hurricane relief effort "Trump's Katrina." In reality Krugman did write this, realized his factual mistake, and posted a retraction within six hours. This is not fake news. This is an error and a prompt correction. To label it *fake news* is an attempt to equate it falsely with Trump's consistent efforts to invalidate any media story he doesn't like (the vast majority of which are accurate).

Moreover even using the term *fake news* in a non-ironic way (unless quoting Jon Stewart's description of his old Comedy Central broadcast *The Daily Show*) demonstrates the user's implicit agreement with Trump that legitimate media outlets intentionally and persistently lie in their reporting about the president. This is dangerous rhetorical drivel coming from a conservative journalist purporting to be a truth-teller. It supports Mr. Trump's authoritarian attempts to delegitimize the Fourth Estate as a whole and as wholly imperative to democracy.

The next thing you know, Donald will try to shut down news outlets he doesn't like. Oh, wait — he tweet-threatened *NBC News* with pulling their broadcasting license just yesterday. (Worse yet, he said they were as bad as *CNN*. Dis or badge of honor?)

B) Attempts to Foist False Equivalency on Journalists

The other example of false equivalency involves the demand that journalists maintain strict neutrality even when the two (or more) sides of the story obviously do not carry equal veracious weight.

Continetti chides mainstream journalists for being "trapped in a condition of perpetual outrage, seizing on every rumor of discontent and disagreement, [and] reflexively denouncing Trump's every utterance and action." He was "stunned" to read Pew Research Center reporting that in the president's first 60 days in office, 62% of news stories leaned negative against Trump compared to Obama's (20%), (George W.) Bush's (28%), and Clinton's (28%) first two months.

"This, at a time when the stock market is at record highs, the economy is at full employment, and Americans are upbeat about the recovery. The president's inability to register majority approval in opinion polls may be unprecedented, but so is the amount of negative coverage he has received. Perhaps there's a connection."

(Ibid.; Continetti; 10/7/2017.)

You're damn right there's a connection, Matthew. The president's unprecedented low approval ratings are proportional directly to his unprecedented poor behavior and job performance. Sure, Obama's economic recovery still is kicking butt (in spite of Trump) nine months after he left office. But even if you mistakenly credit Donald 100% for the economic good times, that does not offset the incompetence, immaturity, and immorality he has demonstrated consistently through 60, 180, or 270 days in.

Apparently by Continetti's standards, President Trump should be achieving at least 50% positive media coverage all the time. If that were the case, it *would* represent a false neutrality or false equivalency. If the mainstream media did that, they *would* be lying. They *would* be reporting from behind what he calls a pre-Trump "pretense of objectivity and detachment."

This is what makes Mr. Continetti's longing for equivalency false. If *neutral* means negative coverage must be balanced by a commensurate amount of positive coverage, then in Trump's case the media would have to lie (including withholding truth) to be neutral. Because President Trump's negative-positive ratio of *performance* is nowhere near 50-50.

You want *stunning*? The figure of 62% negative coverage in Trump's first 60 days seems stunningly low to me. The media must have been overcompensating to be fair because the president caught them off guard with his colossal boorishness and incompetence. The guy has been a dangerous failure. Of *course* Obama's and Bush's and Clinton's negative numbers were way below that — they didn't scare the bejesus out of women, minorities, and U.S. allies. It is astonishing — *stunning* — how my attitude toward George W. Bush has softened since President Trump's inauguration.

Astonishing, stunning, and frightening. Donald Trump has changed the outrage paradigm (another good word). He rapidly is desensitizing us to his outrageousness and mendacity, his *prevaricatum verbosium*. And this is his strategy. Trump cares nothing about policy or — to quote Sen. Al Franken (D-Minn.) quoting one of his role models, the late Sen. Paul Wellstone (D-Minn.) — "[Politics should be about] making people's lives better." For President Trump it's all about ego, self-aggrandizement, and playground put-downs of anyone who does not succumb to his demand for sycophantic loyalty. National security and making people's lives better be damned.

"Trump Does Not Change"

> "Trump does not change, but his critics in the media have. Their feelings of revulsion toward him have deepened. Their eagerness to oppose him has become more acute. The scope of their vision has constricted to include only Trump: what he says, tweets, and does."

> (Ibid.; Continetti; 10/7/2017.)

Mr. Continetti is right about one thing: "Trump does not change." So much for the president's better angels maturing him into the job. Conversely President Trump does change — he's getting worse over time. He's enamored with his Teflon image, which certainly will have its limits.

Of *course* journalists' "feelings of revulsion toward him have deepened." Of *course* "their eagerness to oppose him has become more acute." Journalists are human beings who legitimately are afraid of the damage this president has done and what he ultimately will do if not stopped. Journalistic integrity and great investigative reporting are not guaranteed to abort the Trumpian carnage, but they are our best hope.

I'll be deeply concerned if the overall coverage of Mr. Trump *ever* gets to 50-50, negative-positive, because that would be so far from reality. If we let the desensitization set in, we're in grave danger. Yes, journalists must stay focused on what Trump "says, tweets, and does."

More Sen. Bob Corker

Last week I highlighted Sen. Bob Corker's (R-Tenn.) open criticism of Donald, coming from a highly respected, clear-thinking Republican. Mr. Corker is chair of the Senate Foreign Relations Committee. He was an early supporter of Trump's candidacy and presidency. He was on the short lists for vice president and secretary of state. And he was one of just several senators to forge personal relationships with the president and his family.

Within the first several months of Mr. Trump's tenure, Sen. Corker began reconsidering his position. His words are credible because of his early support and because Donald respected Bob enough to consider him for those two high-level positions. And — they were buds. The president did not double-cross or disrespect Mr. Corker before the senator began his criticism. Bob simply started seeing reality. The president, however, *is* disrespecting Bob Corker these days.

Though Corker voiced some damning criticism a week ago last Wednesday, the president apparently wasn't motivated until the following Sunday morning, by a *Fox News* broadcast, to respond via Twitter:

> "Senator Bob Corker 'begged' me to endorse him for reelection in Tennessee. I said 'NO' and he dropped out (said he could not win without … my endorsement). He also wanted to be Secretary of State, I said 'NO THANKS.' He is also largely responsible for the horrendous Iran Deal! … Hence,

I would fully expect Corker to be a negative voice and stand in the way of our great agenda. Didn't have the guts to run!"

(Trump, Donald, R-N.Y., U.S. president; Twitter post; 10/8/2017.)

Note that all three of the president's tweet-declarations have been debunked, one by public record. Sen. Corker responded:

"It's a shame the White House has become an adult day care center. Someone obviously missed their shift this morning."

(Corker, Bob, R-Tenn., U.S. Senate Foreign Relations Committee chair; Twitter post; 10/8/2017.)

Later that Sunday, Oct. 8, 2017, Sen. Corker participated in a *New York Times* telephone interview with reporter Jonathan Martin. The interview was on the record and knowingly recorded by representatives for both parties. In it Corker apparently confirms what most GOP senators have acknowledged secretly for months: that President Trump is dangerously unfit for office, that most Republican legislators agree with this, and that Trump needs to be controlled for the security of our nation.

"Look, except for a few people, the vast majority of our caucus understands what we're dealing with here. … Of course, they understand the volatility that we're dealing with and the tremendous amount of work that it takes by people around him to keep him in the middle of the road. …

"[President Trump is treating his office like] a reality show … like he's doing 'The Apprentice' or something … [his reckless threats could set the nation] on the path to World War III. …

"[The president] concerns me. He would have to concern anyone who cares about our nation. I know for a fact that every single day at the White House, it's a situation of [senior administration officials] trying to contain him. …

"A lot of people think that there is some kind of 'good cop, bad cop' act underway [with North Korea], but that's just not true. … I know [Trump] has hurt, in several instances, he's hurt us as it relates to negotiations that were underway by tweeting things out. …

"I don't know why the president tweets out things that are not true. You know he does it, everyone knows he does it, but he does."

(Corker, Bob, R-Tenn., U.S. Senate Foreign Relations Committee chair; interview conducted by Martin, Jonathan; The New York Times; 10/8/2017.)

Clearly President Trump is the one who is "somewhere between the hysterical and the lunatic," not the mainstream press. I'm hoping and expecting more Republicans to follow Sen. Bob Corker's brave lead until we have a healthy flow of GOP eye-opening. Matthew Continetti, mainstream media honesty by its nature precludes the foisting of false neutrality or equivalency upon journalists. If the president consistently performs incompetently and unethically, the coverage *will* be lopsided. That is reality. That is integrity. That, 62% of us hope, will save our democracy.■

10/19/17 — Two-Headed Washington Panderer

"During the 2012 [presidential primary] election campaign, I took a phylogenic turn and explored the evolutionary development of the two-headed Washington panderer:

"[Former Sen.] Rick Santorum [(R-Pa.)] is a panderer of the highest two-headed order. Santorum has positioned himself as supporting *and* opposing the war in Afghanistan at the same time. On March 18, 2012, he summed up his position to Jonathan Karl on *ABC's This Week:* 'Let's either commit to winning or let's get out.'

"Karl pressed: 'OK, so what does President Santorum do? Do you commit to winning, and what does that take? Or do you say it's time to get out?'

"Santorum responded: 'Well, I think if you commit to winning, you change the entire dynamic in the region. You change the dynamic with respect to the Taliban, and you recognize that we're going to stay there, and we're going to finish the job.'

"What!? Sen. Santorum wants to give 'respect to the Taliban'!? ...

"Rick's nonresponse to Jonathan Karl — Santorum never answered the question — is the epitome of meaningless, noncommittal doubletalk. Let me translate: 'If you're for the war and want victory for America, I'm with you. If you're against the war and want to bring our troops home now, I'm with you.'

"And Newt Gingrich is saying to himself, 'I can't believe I'm losin' to this guy' *(— thanks to 'Michael Dukakis,' aka Jon Lovitz, 'SNL').*"

(Ersin, Tom; "Unendangered Species: The Two-Headed Washington Panderer"; *Barack vs. the Anti-PC: Laying the Groundwork for a 2016 Donald Trump Presidential Run;* 2017.)

Today we have another quintessential two-headed Washington panderer in the news, but this one is America's chief executive. Here's the thing: I would take a President Santorum over a President Trump any day of the week. And that is the colossally spine-chilling point — Rick Santorum looks good compared to Donald Trump. That scares the "dynamics in the region" out of me.

Art of the (Iran Nuclear) Deal

Last Friday President Trump "decertified" the Iran nuclear deal negotiated by the Obama administration to curtail Iran's nuclear bomb development. The president is obligated to certify (or decertify) every 90 days, based upon U.S. inspectors' reports, that Iran is complying with the deal. In return, America maintains the lifting of stringent economic sanctions on Iran.

Note that almost all of Trump's top advisers have declared Iran in compliance and that it is a good deal; they've advised the president to keep his nose out of it. But in Donald's mind it has Barack Obama's fingerprints and it must go. Behind-the-scenes reporting says the president has been throwing fits about continuing the deal and wants to cancel it outright. But in this "adult daycare" White House *(— thanks to Sen. Bob Corker, R-Tenn.),* chief of staff Gen. John Kelly and others have quelled Trump's tantrums just enough by convincing him to decertify rather than pull out.

Then Trump held a news conference in which, as the reporting analogy goes, *he punted* to Congress. He said it's now Congress' responsibility to "fix" the deal within 60 days or he might still pull out.

The beauty of all this for a shifty, uninformed leader like Trump is that he's positioned both of his pandering heads to project blame and take credit no matter which way the wind ends up blowing. And he looks (panderingly) tough to his base of supporters.

Here are the possible scenarios. 1) If Congress doesn't fix the deal, and President Trump *pulls out*, and Iran gets the bomb: It's Congress' fault for not acting. 2) If Congress does nothing, and Donald succumbs to his generals' pressure and *stays in*, and Iran gets the bomb: It's Congress' fault for not acting. 3) If Congress *changes* the deal, causing the *U.S.* to be out of compliance, and Iran gets the bomb: It's Obama's fault for making a bad deal. 4) If the deal holds and Iran doesn't get the bomb: Trump takes credit — just because.

On a lighter note, consider how all this looks to Kim Jong Un as he contemplates making a deal with Trump to curtail North Korea's nuclear ambitions. Kim gets news (even though his people don't). He's watching the Iran deal. He knows about Donald's multiple bankruptcies and Trump's callous stiffing of numerous contractors big and small. Kim sees the president as an unstable deal-*breaker*.

Donald Trump is neither tough nor a good dealmaker; he's a two-headed Washington panderer.

Some of My Best Friends Are Republicans

This past Monday President Trump (R-N.Y.) and Senate Majority Leader Mitch McConnell (R-Ky.) held a hastily contrived news conference to show the world how much they love each other. I included the obvious political affiliations to underscore that they are in the same party. In recent months McConnell has referenced Trump's "excessive expectations" surrounding the legislative process. The president has responded — with caricaturistic (*and,* sadly, characteristic) overkill — by mercilessly tweet-trashing McConnell (and other Republicans) for the failure to get Obamacare repeal-and-replace through the Senate.

Apparently Trump and McConnell have regrouped and called a truce. Although if ever a public display of acquiescence personified the joke about looking like a hostage video, Mitch's performance Monday was it. The president has no trouble turning on a dime if it will benefit him (in this case, strengthening the chances of getting his first legislative win: tax "reform"). In fact Trump relishes his Oscar-worthy performances. He loves to infuriate critics by successfully manipulating his base, good governing be damned.

President Trump attacks legislators in his own party almost as much as he attacks Democrats. But when he needs them, it's as if the attacks never occurred. Look at his relationship with Sen. John McCain (R-Ariz.). One of Trump's pandering heads attacks John's war record. The other Trump head praises him when his vote is needed — then hands back to the first head to trash the senator when John doesn't vote Donald's way. The president wishes him well after McCain's recent brain cancer diagnosis. Then when McCain publicly questions generic "half-baked spurious nationalism," Donald threatens to attack him and "it won't be pretty."

This is two-headed Washington pandering of the highest order.

Cost-Sharing Reductions

The president signed an order last Friday to undercut the Affordable Care Act further by stopping "cost-sharing reductions," which significantly lower health care deductibles and copayments for Americans of lesser means. He's already drastically cut funds to distribute enrollment information and cut access to the ACA sign-up website. And he frequently makes declarations such as "Obamacare is dead" or "Obamacare has collapsed" knowing many Americans will take him literally and not attempt to sign up.

The nonpartisan Congressional Budget Office says that the president stopping CSRs will raise health care premiums 20% by 2018 and 25% by 2020, increase the federal deficit $194 billion by 2026, and eliminate all health care exchange options for 5% of the U.S. population.

Trump's intention is to put his jackboot on the ACA's neck and suffocate it by significantly raising premiums and depressing enrollment. Obamacare helps many low-income and middle-class citizens. But once again, this time literally, it has former President Obama's name all over it so it must go.

The following Tuesday, Senators Lamar Alexander (R-Tenn.) and Patty Murray (D-Wash.) announced they had reached an agreement on bipartisan health care legislation they had been working on in various forms for months. Along with some reasonable concessions for Republicans the bill would continue CSRs for two years.

Later that day in a joint news conference with visiting Greek Prime Minister Alexis Tsipras, one of the U.S. president's pandering heads said he supported the "short-term solution so that we don't have this very dangerous little period" (the dangerous period his order would cause). Trump called the bill "a very good solution." He seemed to take partial credit by saying he had been involved with its development.

Then — the next day — President Trump's other head did a tweet-backtrack:

> "I am supportive of Lamar as a person & also of the process, but I can never support bailing out ins co's who have made a fortune w/ O'Care."
>
> (Trump, Donald, R-N.Y., U.S. president; Twitter post; 10/18/2017.)

The second half of this tweet is disgustingly dishonest on its two faces: 1) Trump is misrepresenting the payments as insurance company payoffs rather than the low-income subsidies they are; and 2) the president is feigning umbrage toward insurance companies making more money when in fact, by killing Obamacare, he happily will be giving his executive brethren exactly what they want: the ability to profit more and be restricted less.

The hypocrisy is breathtaking. Again Donald has put himself in a position to land on either side of the fence, take credit either way, and project blame in whichever direction will help him.

President Trump is a pandering two-headed panderer — who is redundantly panderous.

Hug an Investigative Reporter

On Sunday night, *CBS' 60 Minutes* devoted two of its standard three segment slots to a joint investigation it did with *The Washington Post* on a story related to the opioid crisis. The *Post* ran its piece the next day. The story of opioid epidemic deaths is bad enough. But the *60 Minutes/Post* exposé detailed the cynical sacrifice of tens of thousands of opioid/heroin overdose victims for pure greed. (When opioid addicts can't get their pills, they often turn to heroin — and often overdose.)

Well after the existence of the problem was known widely, Rep. Tom Marino (R-Pa.) took many generous big pharma campaign donations to pass a law that would weaken the federal Drug Enforcement Agency's ability to flag and stop unusually large drug company shipments of opioids. Huge portions of these questionable shipments end up on the street and in shady doctors' hands under the guise of "pain clinics."

Rep. Marino tried and failed for a few years to get his bill passed. In 2016 he and several other members of Congress finally succeeded in hoodwinking the Justice Department to go along with the industry-friendly relaxation of opioid regulations. The DEA vigorously had opposed these efforts for several years but ultimately had a leadership change and relented. This paved the way for sneaking the legislation through Congress.

Democrats and the Obama administration are not without responsibility. It appears this bill was rushed through the system under the ruse of helping patients in pain, with few legislators, Justice Department officials, or White House staff taking a good look at it. The sickening truth emerged only after Joe Rannazzisi — a former high-ranking DEA agent who was horrified by the extraordinary number of drug overdoses — and others blew the whistle to the *60 Minutes/Post* investigators.

Here's the kicker: Rep. Tom Marino, until Tuesday, was President Trump's nominee for White House drug czar. Yes, take that in. One pundit this week included Marino as an example of the administration's poor vetting of candidates for top jobs. But I agree with Nick Confessore of *The New York Times* who said this week on *MSNBC's MTP Daily* that Tom Marino was vetted perfectly: President Trump chose exactly the kind of candidate he wanted to oversee drug policy and regulation. He chose the kind of rich-business-executive-friendly candidate Trump has chosen for the majority of important White House posts.

But investigative reporting happened. For all of Donald's (I hate even to repeat the term) *fake news* accusations, the Fourth Estate is exhibiting its indispensability more than any time since the Watergate era. If not for investigative reporters, disgraced Gen. Michael Flynn still would be national security adviser, reporting back to Turkey and Russia. Former Trump campaign Chair Paul Manafort would be embedded somewhere high up in the administration, under Ukrainian and Russian oligarchal influence. Former Trump HHS Secretary Tom Price still would be flying extravagant charter flights at taxpayer expense. And Ivanka's shoe line still would be producing designer pumps in Chinese sweatshops. Oh, wait — that never stopped.

Ultimately Rep. Marino was exposed, and Trump ordered him to withdraw from consideration. But the president knew who he had all along. Without the investigative spotlight, Donald was happy to continue populating the swamp with the swampiest of creatures ready to benefit his rich peers at the expense of the little people.

Once his nominee was soiled publicly, Trump's other pandering head popped up to show faux empathy for the poor drug addicts.

————————

And all of that is just this week.

————————

The two-headed Washington panderer:

> "Though not well known by its scientific classification, this variety of bipedal primate is spotted periodically throughout the United States. … The ubiquitous Washington panderer is a subspecies of Homo sapiens politicus, which itself is a subspecies of Homo sapiens, of the genus Homo. … This mammal [can be] a cute, cuddly creature while pandering … [At other times] it exhibits aggressive, vicious, and fiercely territorial behavior."
>
> (Ibid.; Ersin; 2017.)

Donald Trump is the most panderous (and venomous) of the two-headed Washington panderers. He is a panderer of the highest two-headed order.■

10/26/17 — Who Will Be the Edward Brooke of the Trump Era?

We must never forget that our current president tweets — he *tweets* — daily insults like a 15-year-old Valley girl lying about her former BFF who just stole her boyfriend:

> "Bob Corker, who helped President O give us the bad Iran Deal & couldn't get elected dog catcher in Tennessee, is now fighting Tax Cuts.... ... People like liddle' Bob Corker have set the U.S. way back."
>
> (Trump, Donald, R-N.Y., U.S. president; Twitter posts; 10/24/2017.)

This is not a Donald aberration. It's solidly characteristic of President Trump's colossal lack of intellect, veracity, and maturity. We must never forget this, nor take it for granted, nor make it normal in any way.

In other news, First Lady Melania Trump visited a Detroit middle school this week for a stop on her anti-cyberbullying tour. She told students, "I always believe that you need to treat each other with respect and kindness and compassion, but also stay true to yourself."

After her spewing of some of the most vacuous pabulum this side of "Just say no," it's not immediately clear if the first lady knows to whom she is married.

Let me offer some presidential fact-checking. First, Bob Corker opposed the Iran nuclear deal *(— true)*. Second, Sen. Corker could be elected dogcatcher easily in Tennessee, or Georgia or Alabama. He is renowned across the tri-state area for his animal control credentials *(— writer's embellishment)*.

George Will: "Trump's Poodle" and Other Cool Analogies

> "With eyes wide open, Mike Pence eagerly auditioned for the role as Donald Trump's poodle. Now comfortably leashed, he deserves the degradations that he seems too sycophantic to recognize as such. … Pence is a reminder that no one can have sustained transactions with Trump without becoming too soiled for subsequent scrubbing."

> (Will, George, conservative opinion writer; "Sinister Figures Lurk Around Our Careless President"; *The Washington Post;* 10/13/2017.)

George Will is prescient.

Chief of staff Gen. John Kelly is the person placed in Trump's daily orbit whose unquestioned integrity was supposed to offset the president's galactic lack thereof. A week after the *Post* published Will's article, Kelly trotted out — or was trotted out — to the White House press podium to defend Donald's botched condolence call to a fallen (killed in Niger) Green Beret's widow and Trump's subsequent lies about that call.

The widow, Myeisha Johnson, other family members, and longtime family friend Rep. Frederica Wilson (D-Fla.) were in a limo en route to receive the body of Sgt. La David Johnson, killed in an ambush Oct. 4, 2017, when the president called. (Reporters had asked him the day before about the four U.S. casualties in Niger; he subsequently rushed to make condolence calls he hadn't planned on making.) Ms. Johnson chose to put the president on speakerphone so all in the vehicle could hear. After some niceties Trump said something to the effect of, "Well, he knew what he was signing up for, but I guess it hurts anyway." The family was offended and hurt by his words and tone. Rep. Wilson related the call to the press. Trump repeatedly denied he said those words and initiated an eight-day tweet-putdown offensive on "wacky" Congresswoman Frederica Wilson.

No one accused the president of intentionally offending the family; he simply bungled the call. Nevertheless the family was offended — that's what they felt. After Donald denied saying those words, Kelly implicitly conceded that Trump *did* say those words though unartfully (Kelly and others also had listened in on the call from Trump's end). If Gen. Kelly had left it there he would have been OK. But then he slandered Rep. Wilson for "secretly" listening in on the call and accused her of statements she never made at a 2015 FBI building dedication.

The refutatious proof came out immediately: 1) the widow chose to put the call on speakerphone (as was her absolute right); and 2) a forgotten video of the congresswoman's 2015 speech surfaced in which she *never* took credit for obtaining funding for the building (as Kelly had accused) and effusively praised — not herself but — fallen FBI agents, the FBI in general, first responders, and GOP legislators who helped her get the facility officially named in time for the ceremony. Uh-oh.

Trump's entire premise for his weeklong assault on Rep. Frederica Wilson was that she secretly listened in on the call, she lied about his words to Myeisha Johnson, she was self-serving, and she wore cowboy hats. Then Sgt. Johnson's mother confirmed the call's speakerphone status and that Trump said those words. Then Sgt. Johnson's widow confirmed Trump said those words. Then the video of Rep. Wilson's dedication speech materialized. Then Gen. Kelly never apologized for slandering Wilson nor did he correct the record.

Rep. Wilson occasionally does wear cowboy hats. One out of four ain't bad.

John Kelly's days in the White House are numbered. He officially is a "Trump poodle," a la Mike Pence and Sean Spicer, and has become "too soiled for subsequent scrubbing." He will leave due to terminal humiliation. But there is one way for Kelly to redeem himself: He could follow in the footsteps of Sen. Bob Corker who said this week that his early support of Donald Trump was a mistake and that the president is hurting our democracy and literally endangering our country. C'mon, Gen. Kelly, you can do it.

To Be (Ethical), or Not to Be (Ethical)

Many people across the political spectrum like to say you can't legislate morality. A better way to put this might be that you can't legislate *all* morality. Certain things are understood universally to be right or wrong. Trying to legislate all common sense moral issues would clog up legislatures and law books beyond functionality.

How about presidential ethics and ethical norms? Can you legislate those?

Specific ethics-promotion laws were passed after the Watergate imbroglio. With the Freedom of Information Act it became much harder to hide government documents that might show wrongdoing. The Presidential Records Act made Oval Office records the official public property of the U.S. government, not the principals, and established laws for the management of those materials. Campaign finance reform was passed to minimize the influence of money on presidential candidates after they were elected.

In looking back on the prosecution of the Vietnam War, Congress passed the War Powers Act, intended to prevent presidents from continuing indefinite American military combat campaigns without Congress' approval.

Other guidelines — such as releasing tax returns, placing assets in a blind trust, and lying less than, say, 50% of the time, to name a few — have continued to hold by honorable tradition. Until now: the Trump era.

Tax Returns

Donald Trump has refused to release his tax returns as a candidate or as president. If a presidential candidate hides his (or her) income tax returns, he likely is hiding information we need to know about his ability to govern ethically. After President Trump resigns, this will have to be legislated.

Emoluments

Donald Trump continues to accept payments to his businesses from foreign governments and companies. The Constitution has foreign and domestic emoluments clauses, which are supposed to address this, but the GOP-controlled Congress has not been interested in enforcement. After President Trump resigns, this will have to be legislated.

Justice Department

The Department of Justice is supposed to be fiercely independent of the White House. But President Trump has tried persistently to bully the DOJ into submission. He has conducted outrageous, though technically not illegal, personal interviews with three (and only those three, out of over 90) U.S. attorneys who, if confirmed, would have jurisdiction over him and his businesses. And all three of those candidates have ties to Donald. After President Trump resigns, this will have to be legislated.

Blind Trusts

Donald Trump continues to profit by overlapping his business entities with the presidency. The Secret Service, for example, has paid scads of money (reportedly at sometimes inflated rates) to his Mar-a-Lago Florida resort, Trump Tower in New York, and Trump National Golf Club in Bedminster, New Jersey, to house its agents while the president visits. And that's just the iceberg tip. Blind trusts normally preclude presidents from knowing what their assets are and how they are profiting from them. This prevents making presidential decisions for self-enrichment. After President Trump resigns, this will have to be legislated.

Because of the Trump-Russia collusion investigation by three congressional committees and special counsel Robert Mueller, most of Donald's close White House associates need legal representation. The president has made plans to pay $430,000 for some of their legal fees. Obviously this could influence Trump associates' testimony. Moreover the Trump reelection campaign reportedly has paid over $1 million for Donald's and Don Jr.'s Russia-related legal fees. After President Trump resigns, this will have to be legislated.

George Will Concedes: This Author Was Right

> He lies when it's hot, and also lies when it's cold. He lies to
> the young, and likewise lies to the old. He's illegit. He's unfit.

> *(— apologies to Dr. Seuss)*

Additionally, the president lies. This one will be harder to legislate.

On *NBC's Meet the Press* last Sunday, Helene Cooper of *The New York Times* said, "There used to be a time where as president, you knew … you cannot come out and make demonstrably false statements."

Danielle Pletka of the conservative think tank American Enterprise Institute (and abrasive Trump apologist) interrupted: "You mean like, 'I did not sleep with that woman'? That kind of demonstrably false statement?"

First, Danielle, Bill Clinton's words were, "I did not *have sexual relations* with that woman." Get your holier-than-thou, snippy retorts straight. Second, Ms. Cooper acknowledged that Clinton's lie was unacceptable and he suffered huge consequences for it. Third, it was not known — demonstrably — at the time that Clinton was lying. But Trump has said a hundred things that everyone knows are "demonstrably false" as he says them.

And "huge consequences" is an understatement: For that lie President Bill Clinton was impeached. So yes, Ms. Pletka, we simply want commensurate consequences for Mr. Trump. If Bill was impeached once, Donald should be impeached about a hundred times. That's silly, I know. But Danielle got my blood boiling. Danielle Pletka is one of the many conservatives who still seem to believe the (Trumpian) ends justify the (Trumpian) means.

> "Until recently, [Sen. Bob] Corker, an admirable man and talented legislator, has been, like many other people, prevented by his normality from fathoming Trump's abnormality. Now Corker says what could have been said two years ago about Trump's unfitness.
>
> "The axiom that 'Hell is truth seen too late' is mistaken; damnation deservedly comes to those who tardily speak truth that has long been patent. Perhaps there shall be a bedraggled parade of repentant Republicans resembling those supine American communists who, after Stalin imposed totalitarianism, spawned the gulag, engineered the Ukraine famine, launched the Great Terror, and orchestrated the show trials, were theatrically disillusioned by his collaboration with Hitler: You, sir, have gone too far."

(Ibid.; Will; 10/13/2017.)

We don't agree on many things, but George Will has backed me up on this from the beginning of Donald's candidacy: We both predicted a President Trump would be a debacle "such as the world has never seen" (*— thanks to Donald Trump*). We both knew he was dangerously unfit for office.

On the Senate floor this week, Sen. Jeff Flake (R-Ariz.) made a dramatic, full-bore condemnation of Donald Trump's "colossal lack of intellect, veracity, and maturity" (to quote myself). Sadly it was combined with his announcement that he will not seek reelection in 2018 because there currently is no room in today's Republican Congress for a conservative with integrity.

Mr. Will, Mr. Flake, and other vertebrate Republicans will need to be the ones to save American democracy from a 70-year setback. Those two saw it coming from the beginning. Senators Bob Corker and John McCain finally have come around, better late than never.

The Trump presidential yacht has sprung its initial leaks. The next big milestone will be when the first GOP senator calls for the president's resignation. Flake and Corker are so close. For obvious reasons, the calls to resign must originate within the president's own party to be effective.

On Nov. 4, 1973, Sen. Edward Brooke of Massachusetts became the first Republican senator to call for GOP President Richard Nixon's resignation. Nixon resigned Aug. 8, 1974. Who will be the Edward Brooke of the Trump era?

> "Unless someone like you cares a whole awful lot, Nothing is going to get better. It's not."
>
> (Geisel, Theodor ["Dr."] Seuss; *The Lorax;* 1971.)∎

Quotes of the Week

> "Most average Republicans are throwing up over the fact the [congressional GOP] knuckleheads are running the show."
>
> (Boehner, John, R-Ohio, former U.S. House speaker; interview conducted by Heath, Ryan; Frankfurt, Germany; *Politico Brussels Playbook;* 10/26/2017.)

"If we can teach young people, and people generally, not to start [taking opioids], it's really, really easy not to take 'em."

(Trump, Donald, R-N.Y., U.S. president; national address; White House; 10/26/2017.)

11/02/17 — Stupid or Sleazy? – or Both?

I haven't commented a lot on the Trump-Russia investigation. The president's sheer incompetence, mendacity, and ethical paucity have overshadowed the nebulous nature of the collusion probe.

Until now.

Bob Mueller Is a Republican Appointed by Republicans

Before this week, little was known about what special counsel Robert Mueller might turn up in the investigation of possible Russian-American collusion to interfere with the 2016 U.S. presidential election. This speaks to the integrity and discipline of his investigation. Despite some Republicans' and conservative pundits' phony accusations of bias, Mueller is running an airtight, nonpartisan campaign to get to the truth about the Russia question.

Moreover Bob Mueller is a Republican, appointed by a Republican president (George W. Bush) to be acting deputy attorney general, then director of the FBI where he served for 12 years. Last May Trump's own deputy attorney general — a Republican — appointed Mueller to head the special counsel Russia investigation.

Mr. Mueller dropped the first indictments Monday, only five months after his appointment. This was explosive because it confirmed there were significant indictments to drop. (Trump supporters predicted and hoped there would be none.) Most pundits and legal experts agree this is a strong indication that the investigation is moving promptly and thoroughly, uncovering a lot of fertile ground.

This week we learned former Trump campaign Chair Paul Manafort probably laundered tens of millions of dollars and made several offshore bank transfers of close to $1 million each for fancy rugs, fancy clothes, and landscaping services. (That must be *some* lawn.) These were included in a long list of Paul's other previously secret personal transactions. The secrecy was to avoid paying U.S. taxes on questionably earned income. We know many millions of dollars changed hands between Mr. Manafort and Russian oligarchs with close ties to President Putin.

We also learned Trump campaign foreign policy adviser George Papadopoulos made overtures to Russian contacts to pursue hacked Clinton campaign emails, and that Trump campaign superiors gave him attaboys for his "great work." (He accepted a plea bargain related to perjury charges and has been cooperating with Mueller for several months.) We learned George knew about the trove of "thousands" of Clinton campaign Russian-hacked emails *before* the world knew about them. We know Trump campaign Co-Chair Sam Clovis encouraged Papadopoulos' contacts with the Russians. And we know Sam reportedly also is cooperating with Mueller's investigation.

This was just Robert Mueller's opening move.

Innocent, Though Proven Incompetent

Let's assume Donald Trump, himself, is innocent of authorizing or knowing about any Russian collusion. (Just play along for a minute.) The headlines this week alone provide enough evidence supporting the president's incompetence and ethical deficiencies to trigger the 25th Amendment: Namely, he appoints shady, swampy people to work for him, he's endangering U.S. national security, he can't run an organization, and he cannot not tell a lie.

Several incarnations of the *stupid-or-sleazy?* theme in relation to the Trump administration's actions have been circulating through the late-night talk show landscape since Inauguration Day. It is an apt framing of many of those actions. It distills them to one of only two possible explanations, neither of which is pretty. For our purposes, *sleazy* includes *immoral, unethical, illegal,* or *inhumane.*

"Puerto Rico Cancels Controversial Whitefish Energy Contract to Repair Its Power Grid" (10/29/2017)

Whitefish Energy was granted a no-bid $300 million contract to repair Puerto Rico's electrical grid in the wake of Hurricane Maria. The two-year-old company had two employees on staff the day before the storm devastated the U.S. territory. Whitefish's billed expenses run much higher than those of similar businesses. Whitefish Energy is located in Whitefish, Montana, which is the hometown of Ryan Zinke, head of the U.S. Department of Interior. Zinke and the CEO know each other. Zinke's wife and the CEO's wife are friendly on Facebook. Zinke's son had a summer job with the company. (Mufson, Steven & Hernandez, Arelis R. & Davis, Aaron C.; "Puerto Rico Moves to Cancel Contract With Whitefish Energy to Repair Electric Grid"; *The Washington Post;* 10/29/2017.)

Whitefish Energy appears woefully unqualified for the job. FEMA now is looking at how this got by them. The contract was awarded as mentioned without any other bids. The CEO and Trump's interior secretary are from the same small Montana town, and the two families appear friendly. At the very least there was poor decision-making and an appearance of artifice. Stupid or sleazy?

"U.S. Court Reverses President's Transgender Troop Ban He Announced by Tweet" (10/30/2017)

> "After consultation with my Generals and military experts, please be advised that the United States Government will not accept or allow ... Transgender individuals to serve in any capacity in the U.S. Military. Our military must be focused on decisive and overwhelming ... victory and cannot be burdened with the tremendous medical costs and disruption that transgender in the military would entail. Thank you"

(Trump, Donald, R-N.Y., U.S. president; Twitter posts; 7/26/2017.)

It was reported widely that the president in fact had *no* consultation with his generals nor anyone else before he put out this tweet. Almost all military officials and civil rights attorneys panned the directive. Had they had a heads-up, his own legal and military teams would have researched the issue and told Mr. Trump it was not good for the military, inhumane, and probably illegal. On Monday a federal judge schooled Donald on the basics of judicial checks and balances. The judge did not say, "Thank you."

President Trump likely made this impetuous communication to please his base. He knew if he consulted the experts they would have nixed it. He might have known he couldn't unilaterally order this, or he could have been testing the limits of his attempted authoritarianism rather than bother to consult Oval Office lawyers. Stupid or sleazy?

"Chief of Staff Gen. John Kelly Says 'Lack of Compromise' Caused Civil War" (10/31/2017)

I wanted to like John Kelly when President Trump first appointed him White House chief of staff. As I said last week, "Kelly is the person placed in Trump's daily orbit whose unquestioned integrity was supposed to offset the president's galactic lack thereof." Alas, his association with Trump apparently has made him damaged goods.

Kelly appeared on Laura Ingraham's debut episode of her *Fox News* show this week. He called Robert E. Lee "an honorable man." He said the Civil War was caused by "the lack of an ability to compromise." He said, "Men and women of good faith on both sides made their stand where their conscience had them make their stand."

Mr. Kelly followed that gem by saying he had nothing to apologize for — and would "never" apologize — regarding last week's slanderous defense of the president in which John (at best) misspoke or (at worst) lied about his characterization of Rep. Frederica Wilson (D-Fla.), her statements at a 2015 FBI building dedication, and her "secretly" listening in on a Trump condolence call to a fallen soldier's family.

John Kelly lied or misspoke, was proved wrong, and refused to correct the record. After that, Kelly felt emboldened enough to sympathize with the Confederacy because the darn United States government just would not compromise enough on the South's right to enslave and abuse human beings. Stupid or sleazy?

"Sam Clovis' Agriculture Nomination Suffers Russia Setback; and He's Unqualified" (10/31/2017)

President Trump nominated his campaign Co-Chair Sam Clovis to be the Department of Agriculture's chief scientist, aka undersecretary of agriculture for research, education, and economics. Now that Clovis likely is to be implicated in possible Russian collusion, this nomination is in grave doubt: First, because any scent of Russian contact would remind everyone of the scandal, and second, because as journalist Lawrence O'Donnell (*MSNBC*) explained this week, Trump never will allow Senate Agriculture Committee Democrats a confirmation hearing forum to question Clovis about his contacts with subordinate George Papadopoulos — the same George Papadopoulos who plea-bargained perjury charges and has been cooperating with the Mueller investigation for several months.

Oh, one more thing: Sam Clovis is not a scientist.

Stupid or sleazy?

"Apparent ISIS Lone Wolf Terrorist Attack Kills 8 on Lower Manhattan Bike Path" (10/31/2017)
"Trump Politicizes Terror Attack, Blames Schumer for Visa Program Chuck Tried to Kill" (11/1/2017)

President Trump could not wait even 24 hours — could not wait for all the victims to be identified — before attempting to turn the lower Manhattan terrorist attack that killed eight bicyclists into sick, selfish, political advantage for himself.

> "The terrorist came into our country through what is called the 'Diversity Visa Lottery Program,' a Chuck Schumer beauty. I want merit based. ... We are fighting hard for Merit Based immigration, no more Democrat Lottery Systems. We must get MUCH tougher (and smarter). ... Senator Chuck Schumer helping to import Europes problems' said Col.Tony Shaffer. We will stop this craziness!"
>
> (Trump, Donald, R-N.Y., U.S. president; Twitter posts; 11/1/2017.)

While it is true that *Rep.* Chuck Schumer (D-N.Y.) introduced the visa program bill in 1990, that bill passed Congress with a bipartisan majority and was signed by President George H. W. Bush (R-Texas). At that time, most Republican (as well as most Democratic) legislators and the GOP administration thought it was a good idea.

But things change. In 2013 the so-called Gang of Eight (four Republican and four Democratic senators — including Schumer) saw the need to eliminate the Diversity Visa Program. They tried to end it through a comprehensive immigration reform plan.

> "Actually, the Gang of 8, including Sen. Schumer, did away with the Diversity Visa Program as part of broader reforms. I know, I was there ... In fact, had the Senate Gang of 8 bill passed the [GOP-controlled] House, it would have ended

the Visa Lottery Program AND increased merit based vi-sas."

(Flake, Jeff, R-Ariz., U.S. senator; Twitter posts; 11/1/2017.)

President Trump clearly knows what Sen. Flake knows. Trump knows this because his aides who researched the Schumer visa lottery connection also would have come across the same exculpatory information. Additionally Donald claims to have been against this program all along. Why did he wait until now to propose getting rid of it?

Donald waits weeks before mentioning the four U.S. Special Forces deaths in Niger at the hands of terrorists Oct. 4, 2017, because it hurts his tough-on-ISIS image. The president took days to say only drivel about the 58 deaths and nearly 500 woundings and other injuries at a Las Vegas outdoor country music concert Oct. 1, 2017, at the hands of an American Caucasian terrorist. And he said nothing about any presidential intentions to prevent similar incidents. In fact his press secretary chastised others for bringing up gun control too soon after the shooting, saying, "There's a time and place for a political debate, but now is the time to unite as a country."

Less than 24 hours after New York's apparent ISIS-related attack, however, the president didn't just talk *policy* too soon. He dug up a wild lie that Democrats are responsible. He wasted no time in condemning U.S. immigration laws and the American judicial system, thereby heartening terrorists worldwide. Apparently it wasn't too soon for that. Furthermore Mr. Trump said "Democrat" instead of "Democratic," an intentional middle-school slight.

Stupid or sleazy? — or both?■

Quotes of the Week

"We need quick justice and we need strong justice — much quicker and much stronger than we have right now. Because what we have right now is a joke and it's a laughingstock. And no wonder so much of this [terrorism] takes place."

(Trump, Donald, R-N.Y., U.S. president; Cabinet meeting; 11/1/2017.)

"I'm not under investigation, as you know. … I'm actually not angry at anybody."

(Trump, Donald, R-N.Y., U.S. president; interview conducted by Haberman, Maggie & Baker, Peter; *The New York Times*; 11/1/2017.)

11/09/17 — "Trumpism Without Trump": Going Down Like Trumpism With Trump

"Ed Gillespie worked hard but did not embrace me or what I stand for."

> (Trump, Donald, R-N.Y., U.S. president; Twitter post; 11/8/2017.) *(referring to the losing Virginia GOP gubernatorial candidate, whom Trump strongly endorsed)*

"This is a tidal wave."

> (Wasserman, David; nonpartisan *Cook Political Report;* as cited in Hohmann, James; "The Daily 202: Anti-Trump Backlash Fuels a Democratic Sweep in Virginia and Elections Across the Country"; *The Washington Post;* 11/8/2017.) *(referring to Tuesday's Democratic wave of off-year election victories)*

"This is a coalition of the decent that rose up yesterday."

> (Schmidt, Steve, R-N.J., 2008 McCain-Palin presidential campaign chief strategist; *MSNBC's Deadline: Whitehouse* with Nicolle Wallace; 11/8/2017.) *(referring to Tuesday's Democratic wave of off-year election victories)*

"We're [still] with Trump."

(Ryan, Paul, R-Wis., U.S. House speaker; interview
conducted by Kilmeade, Brian, radio host; *Fox News;*
11/8/2017.) *(responding to widespread Republican losses
across the country in Tuesday's off-year elections)*

Wave Election

Tuesday was Election Day for many states, cities, and districts
in America. It included Virginia's statewide elections, two
gubernatorial races, many mayoral races, and a few special
elections. The theme of the results? Democrats and diversity won
hugely. Women won big. Latinos and African Americans won big.
LGBTQ candidates won big. Republicans and Trumpism lost —
bigly.

Here's a rundown of some results:

— *Virginia governor:* Ralph Northam (D) over Ed Gillespie
(R) (by 9 points)
— *New Jersey governor:* Phil Murphy (D) over Kim Guandagno
(R) (by 13 points)
— *Virginia lieutenant governor:* Justin Fairfax (D) over Jill
Holtzman Vogel (R) (by 5 points)
— *Virginia attorney general:* Mark Herring (D) over John Ad-
ams (R) (by 7 points)
— *Virginia state House:* (D)'s gain 15-19 seats, maybe majority
(4 seats awaiting recounts or runoffs)
— *Maine ACA Medicaid expansion:* approved (by 20 points)
— *Washington state Senate:* (D)'s gain majority with special
election win
— *Georgia state legislature:* (D)'s gain 2 state House seats
(breaking GOP supermajority) and 1 state Senate seat

— *Utah U.S. House seat:* John Curtis (R) over Kathryn Allen (D) (by 28 points)

Note that the Utah U.S. House district is rated one of the most Republican in the country, so that loss by Democrat Kathryn Allen virtually was predetermined.

This list does not include the many mayoral and other races that went to Democrats, as well as some other interesting (Democratic) highlights: Seattle, Washington, elected its first openly lesbian mayor; St. Paul, Minnesota, voted in its first African American mayor; Minneapolis, Minnesota, elected its first openly transgender council member (who is now the first openly transgender non-Caucasian woman elected to public office in a major American city); Virginia elected Danica Roem, its first openly transgender public official, to the state House — she beat 26-year incumbent (and self-proclaimed "chief homophobe" of Virginia) Robert G. Marshall.

> (data courtesy of Hohmann, James; "The Daily 202: Anti-Trump Backlash Fuels a Democratic Sweep in Virginia and Elections Across the Country"; *The Washington Post;* 11/8/2017.)

Consult your favorite internet search engine for more Democratic, diversity electoral firsts this week.

"Trumpism Without Trump"

The morning after Tuesday's gubernatorial election in Virginia there was much discussion about losing Republican candidate Ed Gillespie's attempt to embrace "Trumpism without Trump." That was the catchphrase throughout the media universe after the closely watched race. Gillespie's campaign tried to walk the line between promoting the worst elements of Trump's policies — anti-immigrant fervor, save-the-Confederate-monuments demagoguery, "some very fine people on both sides" white nationalism — and being seen with Donald, himself.

It didn't work. Democratic, Republican, and nonpartisan pundits are calling Tuesday's result a clear repudiation (and *refudiation* — *thanks to Sarah Palin*) of Trump, the man, as well as what he stands for. Democrats swept the state in what former Virginia GOP Congressman Tom Davis called "an old-fashioned thumping." And Democrats surprised the president in many other cities and districts across the country with mayoral, city council, state representative, and state senatorial victories.

In classic Trumpian fashion, just minutes after the race was called for Gillespie's opponent, the president tried to distance himself from his previous push for Ed by tweeting, "Ed Gillespie … did not embrace me or what I stand for." Trump desperately wants us all to forget that he strongly endorsed Gillespie, repeatedly praised Gillespie, urged voters to turn out and vote for Gillespie, and recorded last-minute, full-throated fearmongering robocalls in support of Gillespie.

Did I mention that President Trump went all in for the loser, Ed Gillespie?

Just Like Trumpism *With* Trump

President Trump's anti-transgender, anti-gay embrace couldn't even protect 26-year incumbent and self-appointed "chief homophobe" Bob Marshall (known for his infamous "bathroom bill"). Openly transgender Danica Roem flipped Marshall's Virginia House seat. Several other (Democratic) members of the LGBTQ community also rode to victory elsewhere in the country. Take that, Trumpism — with or without Trump.

Virginia had its largest voter turnout in an off-year election in 20 years. Democrats were fired up to defeat Donald's policies and send a clear message to the president. His humbuggery about Ed Gillespie not embracing him enough clearly is one of the main components of Trumpism — mendacity — that voters rejected.

Pundits on both sides agreed that Virginia's election results were a referendum on the president. They speculated that had Trump campaigned in Virginia for Ed Gillespie (as President Obama did for Democrat and winner Ralph Northam), Gillespie's loss margin could have been bigger. The overall results shocked Republicans — *and* Democrats, who won more races, by larger margins, than they had dared hope for.

After special election defeats earlier this year, especially in Georgia's 6th (congressional) District, Democrats were disheartened, discouraged. But there's nothing like a wave election in your favor to wash away discouragement.

Mike Huckabee Fun Quotes

Mike Huckabee is a staunch supporter of Donald Trump. The former Arkansas governor's daughter, Sarah Huckabee Sanders, is the president's stalwart, abrasive press secretary. Huckabee Sr. represents the Christian far-right wing of Trumpism even though Donald hasn't been in a church since his baptism, and his Bible still has the cellophane wrapper on it. (I stole that last one, from whom I can't remember.) I include these palate-cleansing Mike Huckabee quotes to illustrate further Trump's racist, xenophobic, Christian-pandering, slave-to-the-NRA, public-school-prayer-would-prevent-massacres policies:

> "TX killer was liberal atheist stopped by Christian NRA instructor with privately-owned firearm when existing gun laws failed to stop him."

> (Huckabee, Mike, R-Ark., 2008 presidential primary candidate, former governor, ordained Southern Baptist minister; Twitter post; 11/7/2017.) *(referring to Nov. 5, 2017, Texas church massacre of 26 worshippers; Caucasian terrorist's religious or political views have not been determined; NRA instructor was 26 worshippers too late)*

"It's time to wake up and smell the falafel."

(Huckabee, Mike, R-Ark., 2008 presidential primary candidate, former governor, ordained Southern Baptist minister; *Fox News* with Bret Baier; 11/13/2016.) *(responding to recent Paris terror attack and in defense of closing U.S. borders to all refugees)*

"We ask why there's violence in our schools, but we've systematically removed God from our schools. Should we be so surprised that schools have become a place of carnage? Because we've made it a place where we don't want to talk about eternity, life, what responsibility means, accountability. ... People say, Why did God let it happen? God wasn't armed. He didn't go to the school. But God will be there in the form of ... hugs and with therapy. ... Maybe we oughta let him in on the front end, and we wouldn't have to call him to show up when it's all said and done on the back end."

(Huckabee, Mike, R-Ark., 2008 presidential primary candidate, former governor, ordained Southern Baptist minister; *Fox News Live;* 12/14/2012.) *(responding to — on the same day of — the Sandy Hook Elementary School massacre in Connecticut of 20 first graders and six educators)*

I'll bet it was a comfort to those first graders' Christian parents that their children were sacrificed to help put God and prayer back in our schools. Mike went on the *Fox News* airwaves and said this before the families could even identify their innocents' bodies. Gov. Huckabee, you are a despicable Christian hypocrite. Yeah, let's "talk about eternity, life, what responsibility means, accountability." I wonder what Jesus would have done.

MAGA Hats for Sale — Cheap

In the fight against the Trump doctrine, two very important events have developed in the past few weeks: Tuesday's elections and special counsel Robert Mueller's indictments.

Donald and his administration are vulnerable on several fronts. First, President Trump's finances and business dealings likely involve much legal misconduct over the years. Second, the evidence for presidential obstruction of justice is growing stronger each day. Third, the evidence for collusion with Russia is growing stronger each day. Finally, the stomach of the American electorate for Trump's divisive policies is growing weaker each day.

Add to this the president's colossal incompetence, deceit, and immorality.

Until recently it was not clear where the Russia investigation was going if anywhere. But Bob Mueller's first indictments, filed Oct. 30, 2017, have brought his work into clear focus, especially for Trump's inner circle. We now have strong indication that new indictments will rise higher and wider into that circle. In my opinion there is a likelihood the president ultimately will resign to avoid impeachment.

Some of my fellow liberal anti-Donald friends are of the mind that it would be best to ride out the Trump presidency for four years because Vice President Mike Pence would be more dangerous: Pence's policies are every bit as deplorable as Trump's, and Pence has the political savvy to get his through Congress.

But my thinking is to get Donald out ASAP for the following reasons: 1) he really could prompt an attack (and subsequent war) by North Korea through his dangerous schoolyard taunting of Kim Jong Un or some other unstable despot; 2) Trump's downfall as soon as possible is imperative to defending truth — truth is under the severest presidential attack in modern times; 3) once Trump is brought down, Pence and Republicans will be weakened and disgraced; and 4) Democrats will take back one or both houses of Congress in 2018, which will thwart any attempted Pence-ian affronts to our (representative) democracy. At least that's what I believe.

President Trump's policies and beliefs about America have been rejected in significant, official referendums for the first time since his inauguration. Before this week, speculation had it that the Trump doctrine was weakening in popularity. Record-low polling approval ratings have indicated his influence is waning. But as politicians often say, the only poll that matters is the election — in this case, *elections*. Every indication is that Trumpism with or without Trump is on its way to defeat.

Granted, this was only one cluster of off-year and special elections. And Democrats could underperform in 2018 — in which case I'll eat a "Make America Great Again" hat. But what do you call a blue wave election in 2017?

A great start.■

Quotes of the Week

"The saddest thing is, because I am the president of the United States, I am not supposed to be involved with the Justice Department. I'm not supposed to be involved with the FBI. I'm not supposed to be doing the kind of things I would love to be doing and I am very frustrated by it."

(Trump, Donald, R-N.Y., U.S. president; interview conducted by O'Connor, Larry; *WMAL's The Larry O'Connor Show*; 11/3/2017.)

"Korean golfers are some of the best on Earth. In fact — and you know what I'm going to say — the women's U.S. Open was held this year at Trump National Golf Club in Bedminster, New Jersey."

(Trump, Donald, R-N.Y., U.S. president; South Korean National Assembly address; Seoul, South Korea; 11/7/2017.)

11/16/17 — The Embarrassment Tour

[TOPICS: Trump Asia tour]

President Donald Trump returned home Nov. 14, 2017, from his 12-day tour of Asian countries: Japan, South Korea, China, Vietnam, and the Philippines. Donald and many other Republicans often falsely accused President Obama of conducting an "Apology Tour" of other countries after his election. This week our new president completed his *Embarrassment Tour.*

World leaders do not respect nor trust President Trump for the same reasons two-thirds of Americans don't. His *Trump: The Art of the Deal* persona has been proved pure fiction. *The Art of Say Anything but Don't Keep Your Side of the Bargain,* however, is rueful reality. Republican congressional leaders know this. Most Trump voters should know this by now if they allowed facts and reality to influence their thinking.

The president lies pathologically. The president is ignorant of the world and governing and has no desire to learn. The president is a moral vacuum. World leaders know this. Authoritarians love this. But even other autocrats know Donald can't be trusted and he probably won't last long. They are patronizing him while biding their time.

Donald also is an overbearing, boorish attention hog. Remember back in May 2017 when he was caught on video childishly pushing Montenegro's Prime Minister Dusko Markovic out of the way so Trump could be front and center for a NATO photo op? Then he struck a moronic I'm-important-and-I'm-supposed-to-be-in-front-and-everyone-knows-that pose? This was one of President Trump's first major appearances on the world stage, and he essentially wet his pants on the dais and insulted NATO's wife. He is America's embarrassing oaf.

Many (of my seven) readers simply will label me a Trump-hater and dismiss my characterizations. But I don't make these lightly. The president is a dangerous embarrassment to the United States and he demonstrates it almost daily. One of my goals is to illuminate some specifics for readers who might not follow the presidency and current events every day or hour. I respect those who can turn it off for a while. But many people need a periodic compilation update. Because we must never make this president's behavior normal, nor take it for granted, nor become desensitized to it. Our government's future depends upon vigilance.

Japan

President Trump arrived in Japan Sunday, Nov. 5, 2017. He kicked off his Asia Embarrassment Tour with a campaign-style rally for American and Japanese troops stationed there. Notably missing from the crowd were MAGA ("Make America Great Again") hats and *Rope-Tree-Journalist* T-shirts (popular among Trump rally-goers). But in standard form Mr. Trump bragged about himself in the guise of bragging about America: "We are back home starting to do, I will tell you — and you're reading, and you're seeing — really, really well … since a very, very special day — it's called Election Day."

Spit it out Mr. President. As prone to do, Trump once again credited himself for the sturdy economy, strong stock market, and declining unemployment rate that his predecessor, President Obama, bequeathed to him. Though there have been some gains since "Election Day," Trump takes credit for the New York Stock Exchange and the Industrial Revolution.

President Trump played golf and ate steaks with Prime Minister Shinzo Abe at Kasumigaseki Country Club *(— true)*. MAGA-style hats were passed out, this time with the cutesy slogan twist "Donald and Shinzo: Make Alliance Even Greater" *(— true)*. The president razzed Abe for not owning his own country club. Donald complained about the slow greens. He snuck three mulligans. And he tried to make a deal with Kasumigaseki to add Trump Steaks,

Wine, and Water to the menu. He would throw in a complementary framed *Time* magazine (counterfeit Trump-graced) cover. *(— writer's embellishment)*

In a classic world-view perspective, a Japanese commentator observed:

> "Prime Minister Abe is called a trainer of wild animals. And the world is watching how he does with President Trump."
>
> (Hirai, Fumio; *Fuji TV;* as cited in Davis, Julie Hirschfeld; "Trump Opens Asia Trip Talking Tough in Campaign-Style Rally"; *The New York Times;* 11/5/2017.)

Also on Sunday, North Korea's government newspaper, Rodong Sinmun, issued a statement: "We warn Trump's coteries once again. If they want to avoid ruin, do not make reckless remarks."

When asked if President Trump would tone down his normally inflammatory epithets and taunts of North Korean leader Kim Jong Un while visiting the Asian countries, national security adviser H. R. McMaster said, "The president will use whatever language he wants to use, obviously."

That's what we're afraid of, H. R.

South Korea

On Monday afternoon *Air Force One* landed in South Korea. Presidents Donald Trump and Moon Jae-in had lunch with a group of military troops from both countries at Camp Humphreys, which is 60 miles south of the Demilitarized Zone and home to 30,000 U.S. military personnel. Said Mr. Trump, "I had a choice of having a beautiful, very fancy lunch and I said no, I want to eat with the troops and we ate with the troops."

After small talk with the grunts, Trump and Moon had their *real* ("beautiful, very fancy") lunch at the Blue House, the South Korean presidential mansion. Donald was greeted with protesters' signs reading "No War" and "No Trump." To be fair, other people in the street waved South Korean and American flags.

President Trump later commented on the enormous expansion of Camp Humphreys, which will be complete in 2020: "I know what it cost, and it's a lot of money. And I'm sure I could have built it for a lot less."

Mr. Wheeler-Dealer. Always the pitchman. But Donald, they need the toilets to flush and the roof not to leak. This isn't one of your housing projects in Queens.

On Tuesday Mr. Trump spoke to the South Korean National Assembly. After an October 2017 tweet to Secretary of State Rex Tillerson that "he is wasting his time trying to negotiate with Little Rocket Man," Trump appealed to North Korea's softer side with an offer of diplomacy while also warning, "Do not underestimate us. Do not try us."

Orville Schell, an expert in Asia culture and policy, lauded Mr. Trump's speech: "It was hard-hitting, it was coherent, and he stuck to the teleprompter."

Only in the Trump era can "he stuck to the teleprompter" be considered high praise. Translated this means, "Donald stuck to the safe pabulum his speechwriters wrote and didn't adlib anything stupidly provocative that might get us all killed." Apparently Trump advisers have been pleading with him for months not to invoke his customary schoolyard taunts and put-downs of Kim Jong Un. For the moment they have succeeded. Threats of "fire and fury" raining down on "Little Rocket Man" will wait for another day.

> "In spring 2015, about 88% of South Koreans in a Pew Research Center survey said they trusted the American president to 'do the right thing regarding world affairs.' Two years later, that share has fallen to 17%, according to the Center's global attitudes poll."

(Bennett, Brian; "Trump Offers North Korea 'a Path
to a Much Better Future'"; *Los Angeles Times;*
11/7/2017.)

South Korean President Moon Jae-in employed the time-honored
diplomatic tactic most effective with President The Donald: flattery.
Moon rolled out the red carpet and gushed, "You are already making great progress on making America great again."

They are patronizing him while biding their time.

China

"[President-elect Trump should] stop acting like the diplomatic rookie he is."

(*China Daily;* as cited in John, Tara; "China's State
Media Tells Donald Trump to 'Stop Acting Like a
Diplomatic Rookie'"; *Time;* 12/6/2016.)

"The obsession with 'Twitter diplomacy' is undesirable. … It
is commonly accepted that diplomacy is not a child's game
— and even less is it business dealing."

(*Xinhua*, most influential Chinese state-run media; as
cited in Hunt, Katie; "China Tells Donald Trump to
Lay off Twitter"; *CNN.com;* 1/5/2017.)

Such was the backdrop of China's respect for Donald Trump before
his visit.

At a campaign rally in Fort Wayne, Indiana, May 2, 2016, candidate Trump said this: "We can't continue to allow China to rape
our country. And that's what they're doing. It's the greatest theft in
the history of the world." He's repeatedly called its government a
"currency manipulator." These statements are representative of Mr.
Trump's consistent angry sentiments toward China.

But after a two-hour meeting Nov. 9, 2017, with Chinese President Xi Jinping during the Asia tour China stop, President Trump absolutely was gushing about what a smart cookie (sorry, I really needed this term again) China has been in being able to take advantage of America's former leaders during trade negotiations: "I don't blame China. After all, who can blame a country for being able to take advantage of another country for benefit of its citizens? … I give China great credit."

Mr. Trump later told President Xi, "You are a very special man."

A reporter asked Secretary of State Tillerson if Trump was kissing Xi's butt a little too much while in Xi's country. (The reporter referred to being "too deferential.") Tillerson responded, "I didn't detect that at all."

Trump is the classic blowhard who when face-to-face with the object of his ire collapses like the bottom line on a Trump casino profit and loss statement. When the president is in Xi's house, Xi becomes a fellow master of *Trump: The Art of the Deal* and gets nothing but praise from Donald. How much of a butt-kisser *is* this Trump guy?

Continuing the theme of pile-on flattery, Donald and Melania were treated to a Chinese "state visit plus" starting with a lavish government welcome at the Great Hall of the People. They exited the limo to horn players in red uniforms and took in military bands, ceremonial cannon fire, cheering schoolchildren waving colored pom-poms, and a rare personal tour of the Forbidden City by Xi, himself.

Trump and Xi talked trade. They talked North Korea. They vowed to work together in the "spirit of mutual respect and mutual benefit." Yada, yada …

Did I mention that Xi is patronizing Donald while biding his time?

> [FUN FACT:] After returning home, President Trump tried
> to take credit for tough-minded trade deals worth more than

$200 billion, which he claimed to have negotiated during his China stop. But experts in the know say those deals occurred before Trump's inauguration.

Vietnam

"Danang me, Danang me,
They oughta take a rope and hang me"

*(— thanks to "Adrian Cronauer," aka Robin Williams,
"Good Morning, Vietnam," and Roger Miller)*

Issues specific to Vietnam took a backseat during President Trump's Asian tour Vietnam stop. The *People* magazine highlights took place at the meeting of the Asia-Pacific Economic Cooperation forum in Danang, Vietnam. This is where President Trump informally met with Russia's President Putin.

The world was on edge Nov. 11, 2017, wondering if Vladimir would finally 'fess up to getting Donald elected U.S. president. Alas, President Trump relayed the gist of his conversation with Putin to reporters in the press cabin of *Air Force One*: "He said he didn't meddle. He said he didn't meddle. I asked him again. You can only ask so many times. … He said he absolutely did not meddle in our election. He did not do what they are saying he did."

In a right-back-at-ya response at his own news conference, Putin said that President Trump "behaves very appropriately." (Only in the Trump era …)

In other highlights during the flight between Danang and Hanoi, Donald said, "[former FBI Director James] Comey is proven now to be a liar and he is proven now to be a leaker." Regarding former Director of National Intelligence James Clapper and former CIA Director John Brennan, Trump said, "I mean, give me a break, they are political hacks." Trump added, "So you look at it, I mean, you have Brennan, you have Clapper, and you have Comey. So you look at that and you have President Putin very strongly, vehemently says he had nothing to do with them."

Brennan, Clapper, and Comey, representing the entire (17-agency) U.S. intelligence community, issued the January 2017 report that describes Russia's unprecedented interference in the 2016 United States election to promote electoral chaos and help elect Trump. The entire (17-agency) U.S. intelligence community agrees with a "high level of certainty" that Russia attacked our electoral system, and the orders came from its highest levels of government.

President Trump strengthened *his* case by adding that Vladimir Putin "is very, very strong in the fact that he didn't do it. You have President Putin very strongly, vehemently, says he has nothing to do with that. ... Every time he sees me, he says, 'I didn't do that.' And I believe, I really believe, that when he tells me that, he means it. I think he is very insulted by it."

One more thing: "There was no collusion; everybody knows there was no collusion," Trump said. And the [Steele] dossier is "phony." And it's an "artificial Democratic hit job."

And Ted Cruz's dad killed JFK *(— writer's embellishment)*.

As James Hohmann of *The Washington Post* said, President Trump's Putin comments make Trump look weak, naïve, waffling, inconsistent, like he's hiding something, like he undercuts his staff, and like he doesn't trust U.S. intelligence. (Hohmann, James; "The Daily 202: Six Ways Trump's Putin Comments on Asia Trip Erode U.S. Credibility"; *The Washington Post;* 11/13/2017.)

> "Trump and his followers are willing to believe anything because they *want* to believe anything that confirms their counterfactual world. ... It renders Trump susceptible — eager, even — to believe our enemies, even — especially! — at the expense of American values, security, and interests. He's putty in the hands of wily autocrats. He's therefore the type of target that counterintelligence operatives dream of — an arrogant fool."

> (Rubin, Jennifer, conservative opinion writer; "Russia's Mark: A Dangerous Fool for a President"; *The Washington Post*; 11/12/2017.)

Finally, a little more Donald:

> "Believe it or not, even when I'm in Washington or New York, I do not watch much television. I know they like to say that. People that don't know me, they like to say I watch television — people with fake sources. You know, fake reporters, fake sources. But I don't get to watch much television. Primarily because of documents. I'm reading documents. A lot. And different things. I actually read much more."

> (Trump, Donald, R-N.Y., U.S. president; Q&A with reporters; *Air Force One*; 11/11/2017.)

The reporters on *Air Force One* respectfully stifled all spit-takes, guffaws, snickers, and smirks.

Meanwhile President Trump snuck away from his pesky advisers — you know, those advisers mentioned earlier who "have been pleading with him for months not to invoke his customary schoolyard taunts and put-downs of Kim Jong Un":

> "Why would Kim Jong-un insult me by calling me 'old,' when I would NEVER call him 'short and fat?' Oh well, I try so hard to be his friend - and maybe someday that will happen!"

> (Trump, Donald, R-N.Y., U.S. president; Twitter post; 11/12/2017.)

We're all gonna die.

Philippines

> "I just wanted to congratulate you because I am hearing of the unbelievable job on the drug problem. Many countries have the problem, we have a problem, but what a great job you are doing and I just wanted to call and tell you that."
>
> (Trump, Donald, R-N.Y., U.S. president; leaked White House transcript of call to Philippine President Rodrigo Duterte; 4/29/2017.)

Donald Trump is a fan of dictators and authoritarians like Philippine President Rodrigo Duterte. Since taking power, Duterte has overseen a campaign of government-condoned vigilante murders of drug dealers, drug users, and anyone suspected of being either. The *vigilante* part, of course, means all these killings are outside of the Philippine judicial system. Several thousand citizens have been executed under this program since Duterte became president in June 2016. Police operations have carried out over a thousand of those murders with no accountability.

> "Double your efforts. Triple them, if need be. We will not stop until the last drug lord, the last financier, and the last pusher have surrendered or [been] put behind bars — or below the ground, if they so wish."
>
> (Duterte, Rodrigo, Philippine president; State of the Nation speech; 7/25/2016.)

Mr. Duterte also has been implicated in many unsolved murders of journalists during his time as Davao City mayor and Philippine president.

> "The Philippines ranks as the fifth-most dangerous country for journalists, according to a report by the Committee to

Protect Journalists. At least 177 Filipino media workers have been killed since 1986. In the past decade, 42 journalists have been killed with total impunity, the report said, and at least four journalists have been killed in the time since Duterte took office in June 2016."

(Schmidt, Samantha; "Trump Chuckled as Duterte Called Journalists 'Spies.' That's No Joke in the Philippines."; *The Washington Post;* 11/14/2017.)

In short, Rodrigo Duterte has condoned thousands of Philippine murders since he took office a year and a half ago. His police are responsible for many of those, and no one has been held accountable for any of them. Even Kim Jong Un is like, "Whoa, bro, pace yourself."

In a Manila meeting with President Duterte on Monday, Mr. Trump boasted of his "great relationship" with the Philippine strongman. Afterward during a news conference with U.S. journalists, Trump was asked, in front of Duterte, if he had brought up human rights issues in their meeting. Mr. Duterte cut the reporters off, saying, "Whoa, whoa. This is not a press statement. This is the bilateral meeting. ... With you around, guys, you are the spies."

President Trump laughed — and he *never* laughs. Donald has a great relationship with Rodrigo. They're buds now. They can bond and laugh together about believing journalists are rotten spies.

Apparently human rights did not come up in the Trump-Duterte colloquy, in keeping with the president's prominent non-theme throughout his Asia Embarrassment Tour.

President Duterte famously cussed out President Obama last year for Barack's criticism of Rodrigo's bloody vigilante war on drugs. Barack Obama has these old-fashioned notions about human rights and international norms, which don't get in Donald Trump's way. In fact, you know if Obama did it, Trump childishly will do the opposite because he detests his predecessor. Like Mr. Duterte, Mr.

Trump despises Mr. Obama's excellence of character, moral compass, competence, and intelligence.

The new best friends with a "great relationship" found more common ground in addition to their loathing of dirty, no-good spying reporters: During their sleepover at Rodrigo's house, he and Donald gabbed all night about how they hated that b*tch, Barack.

BFFs.■

11/22/17 — Sexual Harassment: Degrees and Patterns

When the news broke Monday about legendary television journalist Charlie Rose being accused of sexual misconduct by eight women, I was crestfallen, dejected, despondent, hangdog, heartsick, mournful, woebegone, and every other synonym I could find in my thesaurus for *depressed*. We love Charlie Rose. His brand of thoughtful journalism is a large part of my defense for why I watch more TV than I should. He is the epitome of gentlemanly, intelligent, critically thoughtful discussion and information dissemination.

Details

Then I read the Nov. 20, 2017, article in *The Washington Post* by Irin Carmon and Amy Brittain. Our beloved Charlie Rose is a pig.

The article is in keeping with the *Post*'s excellent brand of investigative journalism (without which, President Nixon would have finished his second term, and Attorney General Jeff Sessions might still be fetching Diet Cokes for President Trump — oh, wait …).

The article is long, detailed, and airtight. With on-the-record similar accounts by separate women, and multiple confirmations of their contemporaneous reports to people close to them about the harassment, there virtually is no doubt about Charlie's pattern of piggish behavior.

With Mr. Rose's subsequent qualified admission, there *literally* is no doubt.

Here's the thing: It's not that I disbelieved the story when the headlines first emerged. It's just that my affinity for Charlie Rose was kept aloft by not knowing the details. The details are everything. The documented details are what quickly changed my affinity for Rose to disgust. That's why the vast majority of (2018 Alabama senatorial candidate) Roy Moore's supporters won't read the details. More on that later.

I consider myself an observant and empathic man. But after a legion of credible accounts of sexual misconduct by well-known men over the past several months, I admit I had no idea how pervasive this societal cancer is — and clearly not just among celebrities.

Patterns

One might say President Trump got in just under the wire of increased sexual-harassment awareness and raised consciousness. *I* say the tidal wave of sincere women coming out, telling their stories of sexual abuse at the hands of men, and having confidence they will be believed, is a direct backlash to America's anger at Donald having gotten away with murder.

Look at the men with established patterns, some whose politics I agree with (liberals and independents) and some whose politics I don't agree with (conservatives and Republicans): Harvey Weinstein (Hollywood mogul, Democratic donor); Charlie Rose (journalist, *Bloomberg, CBS, PBS*); Glenn Thrush (journalist, *The New York Times*); Louis C.K. (comedian, liberal); Roy Moore (twice-removed Ala. Supreme Court chief justice and current U.S. Senate Republican candidate); Michael Oreskes (journalist, *NPR, The New York Times*); Hamilton Fish (publisher, *The New Republic*); Kevin Spacey (actor, liberal); Mark Halperin (journalist, *NBC*); Leon Wieseltier (editor, *The New Republic*); Rep. John Conyers (D-Mich.); and President Donald Trump (R-N.Y.).

This is a partial list focusing on established patterns of misconduct, courtesy of Sarah Almukhtar, Larry Buchanan, and Michael Gol from their Nov. 21, 2017, article, "After Weinstein: The Fallout for 34 Men Accused of Sexual Misconduct, From Lewd Texts to Rape," in *The New York Times*. As you can see, most of these guys fall on the left side of the political spectrum. Most conservatives purport that *The New York Times* and *NPR* have a liberal slant (though Monica Lewinsky's blue dress and Hillary's emails might dissent with a smirk). And *The New Republic* represents the traditional forefront of liberal media (though its elite star has fallen over the years).

With the exception of Mark Halperin, who can be politically amorphous, the only clear Republicans on this list are Donald Trump and Roy Moore. All the rest are stinkin', rotten, liberal, tree-hugging Democrats who got their comeuppance. Notably, the president holds the current record for documented accusers at 17; Roy Moore probably comes in second with nine including a 14-year-old, a 16-year-old, and other teenaged girls. Doubly notably, Trump and Moore are the only ones on that list *not* to be held accountable so far.

Elections

"Well, he denies it. And by the way, he *totally* denies it."

(Trump, Donald, R-N.Y., U.S. president; Q&A with reporters; White House lawn; 11/21/2017.) *(responding to a reporter asking if a Democrat was worse than a child molester, i.e., Roy Moore, in the U.S. Senate)*

As Catherine Rampell of *The Washington Post* satirically illustrated — in her Nov. 20, 2017, article, "The GOP Readies Itself to Welcome Roy Moore" — prominent GOP politicians are not subject to the same laws of gravity as liberal celebrities in the private sector. As long as the Republican perpetrators deny, deny, deny, their voters are the sole determiners of their fate.

As President Trump has asserted, far-right wing Republican Roy Moore has denied the documented allegations of his — count 'em — nine accusers, therefore *he* must be given the benefit of the doubt.

[FUNNY COINCIDENCE:] Mr. Trump also denies all accusations by his many accusers. Employing faux outrage during the campaign, Donald famously announced that he would sue all of them after the election.

[UPDATE:] No suits have been filed.

Ms. Rampell outlines several instances of conservatives' use of the electoral justification/nullification of sexual harassment:

> *White House press secretary Sarah Huckabee Sanders* — She stated that accusations aimed at President Trump had been covered in depth during the campaign: "We addressed that then. The American people I think spoke very loud and clear when they elected this president."

Donald Trump: Innocent.

> *Sen. Tom Cotton (R-Ark.)* — He was asked if it was time to reevaluate the claims against the president: "Well, it happened in the middle of the campaign last year … and the American people had their say on that."

Donald Trump: Innocent.

> *Fox News' Howard Kurtz* — "We had an election after [candidate Trump was accused]. And he won."

Donald Trump: Innocent.

Roy Moore hasn't been elected U.S. Senator — yet — though Catherine Rampell skillfully lays out the arguments that will be used to defend him if he is victorious.

Defenses

Until then, there are the preelection defenses by many evangelical Christians — *evangelical Christians!* — and Alabama politicians.

The "Sure-he-dated-young-girls-but …" defense:

> "I think that, number one, you need to understand, 40 years ago, what the [social context] was like in Alabama. Judge Roy Moore graduated from West Point and then went on into the service, served in Vietnam and then came back and was in law school. All of the ladies, or many of the ladies that he possibly could have married were not available then, they were already married, maybe, somewhere. So he looked in a different direction and always with the [permission of the] parents of younger ladies … He did that because there is something about a purity of a young woman, there is something that is good, that's true, that's straight, and he looked for that."
>
> (Benham, Flip, pastor; interview conducted by Murphy, Matt & Lindenberg, Andrea; Birmingham, Ala.; *Talk 99.5's Matt & Aunie* [radio show]; 11/20/2017.)

The "I-know-you-are-but-what-am-I" defense:

> "[These accusations are a] war on men. … More women are sexual predators than men. Women are chasing young boys up and down the road, but we don't hear about that because it's not PC."
>
> (Raddish, Franklin, Capitol Hill Independent Baptist Ministries pastor; as cited in Harress, Christopher; "Some Pastors Stand Behind Roy Moore, Cite 'War on Men'"; *AL.com;* 11/18/2017.)

"Where *is* that road?"

> (Colbert, Stephen; *CBS' The Late Show*
> with Stephen Colbert; 11/20/2017.)

The classic "Just-in-case-he-did-it" defense:

"The hypocrisy of Washington has no bounds. So many [are] denouncing Roy Moore when they are guilty of doing much worse than what he has been accused of supposedly doing."

> (Graham, Franklin, evangelical leader, son of Billy; as cited in Herndon, Astead W.; "Why Evangelicals Are Again Backing a Republican Despite Allegations of Sexual Misconduct"; *The Boston Globe;* 11/20/2017.)

"[Alabama Pastor Earl] Wise said he would support Moore even if the allegations were true and the candidate was proved to have sexually molested teenage girls and women. 'There ought to be a statute of limitations on this stuff,' Wise said. 'How these gals came up with this, I don't know. They must have had some sweet dreams somewhere down the line. Plus,' he added, 'there are some 14-year-olds, who, the way they look, could pass for 20.'"

> (Herndon, Astead W.; "Why Evangelicals Are Again Backing a Republican Despite Allegations of Sexual Misconduct"; *The Boston Globe;* 11/20/2017.)

Finally, the "I-do-believe-he-did-it-but-we-need-a-Republican-in-there" defense:

> "I certainly have no reason to disbelieve any of [Roy Moore's accusers ... but] I believe in the Republican Party, what we stand for. ... So that's what I plan to do, vote for Republican nominee Roy Moore."
>
> > (Ivey, Kay, R-Ala., governor; Q&A with reporters; governor's mansion turkey pardon; as cited in Cason, Mike; "Gov. Kay Ivey to Vote for Roy Moore in U.S. Senate Race"; *AL.com;* 11/17/2017.)

Finally, finally, the "I-admit-I-did-it-but-vote-for-me-the-Republican-anyway" defense:

> "I moved on her *(Nancy O'Dell, Billy Bush's Access Hollywood co-host)* and I failed. I'll admit it. I did try and f*** her. She was married. And I moved on her very heavily. ... I moved on her like a b*tch. But I couldn't get there. And she was married. Then all of a sudden I see her, she's now got the big phony t*ts and everything. She's totally changed her look. ...
>
> "I better use some Tic Tacs just in case I start kissing her *(actor Arianne Zucker, who is outside the bus)*. You know I'm automatically attracted to beautiful — I just start kissing them. It's like a magnet. Just kiss. I don't even wait. And when you're a star, they let you do it. You can do anything. Grab 'em by the p***y. You can do anything."
>
> > (Trump, Donald, real estate mogul, reality show actor; private, inadvertent hot-microphone exchange with Bush, Billy, co-anchor of *Access Hollywood*, and seven other *NBC* staff members; celebrity bus, NBC

Studios parking lot, Burbank, Calif.; September 2005.)

These are the Roy Moore supporters who likely have not read the detailed, documented accusations by nine women against the former Alabama Supreme Court judge — you know, that same judge who was removed from the bench twice for violating the Constitution, and the same judge who for five years took a $180,000 annual salary for part-time work from his Christian charity before claiming he hadn't. To be fair, some Alabama citizens, pastors, politicians, and newspapers have denounced Roy Moore or unendorsed him after the sexual-harassment-of-minors charges surfaced. Let's hope they carry some weight.

Al Franken

I can't end this piece without mentioning Sen. Al Franken (D-Minn.) and the accusations against him. Let me give a full disclosure: I loved his work and admired him as a comedian and author, and I love his work and admire him as a force for liberal values in the U.S. Senate.

The strange story of Al Franken is emerging as a test case for examining gray areas in the judgment of admitted sexual harassment committed by a politician.

To recap, Al's first accuser, former model and radio host Lee-ann Tweeden, recently alleged that he forcefully French-kissed her (during a consensual regular kiss) in the course of a comedy skit rehearsal while they were on a 2006 USO tour together. Then a photo was taken on their military flight home showing Al feigning cupping her breasts while she slept and mugging for the camera. (She only saw this photo later and legitimately felt embarrassed, belittled, and humiliated.)

Contrary to the embellishment of conservative commentator Hugh Hewitt, Mr. Franken did *not* keep up a campaign of harassment for two weeks. In fact other photos from that trip showed Al and Leeann appearing friendly. Sen. Franken has apologized profusely for the kiss and the photo and has called for a Senate ethics investigation of his own behavior. Ms. Tweeden publicly has accepted his apology.

The second accuser alleges that Al grabbed her buttocks during a pose with her at the 2010 Minnesota State Fair while her husband snapped the photo. Mr. Franken doesn't recall the incident, says that he's posed for thousands of state fair photos, but still apologizes for the woman feeling disrespected.

Preponderance of the Evidence

Hugh Hewitt has damaged his credibility on this issue (and his truthful reporting in general). On Thursday during *MSNBC's MTP Daily,* he made the assertion that they should *all* not be allowed in Congress — senatorial candidate Roy Moore (R-Ala.), Sen. Al Franken (D-Minn.), and recently accused Rep. John Conyers (D-Mich.) — based on a "preponderance of the evidence." Hugh has been pushing this legal term to judge the veracity of sexual harassment accusers for the past few weeks. A preponderance of the evidence in this case means there is greater than a 50% chance the accusations are true.

Roy Moore? *Check.* John Conyers? A little soon to know for sure but a likely *check.* Al Franken? Definite *check* because Al has 'fessed up and apologized (though Hewitt makes no consideration for Franken's much lesser degree of offenses and lack of established pattern). But when *MTP Daily* host Katy Tur asked Hugh why he voted for Donald Trump in light of the 17 accusers — most of whose stories are documented on the record and their contemporaneous reports corroborated — Hewitt had the arrogance to state the president's accusers did not meet the preponderance of the evidence.

Hugh Hewitt believes there is *less* than a 50% chance that *any* of the multiple Trump accusers are telling the truth. Katy and the two women journalists on her panel politely stifled gasps. Then Tur pointed out that Donald's admission on the *Access Hollywood* video was pretty strong corroboration.

I don't believe in the zero-tolerance, falsely equivalent policy that says if Roy shouldn't be a senator, neither should Al. And don't give me the phony Sarah Huckabee Sanders contention that Al admitted his wrongdoing but Donald and Roy still are innocent until proved guilty. That might fly technically in a court of law but not in the court of common sense.

Degrees and Patterns

Contrary to Hugh Hewitt's self-serving, all-or-nothing standard of guilt, Sen. Franken's example illustrates the need to consider two important factors: 1) the degree of the offenses; and 2) the existence of a pattern of offenses.

Consider the degrees: Roy Moore tried to seduce a 14-year-old girl by sneaking her away from her mother to his house. He threatened to rape a 16-year-old girl in his car, leaving her sobbing on the parking lot pavement of her employer's restaurant when she would not comply with his advances. There are at least seven more accusers with similar stories.

Donald Trump is an admitted serial grabber of women's crotches. He has at least 17 documented, corroborated allegations against him of sexual assault or misconduct.

Al Franken forced a French kiss during a consensual (rehearsal) regular kiss; embarrassed that USO co-volunteer with a crude gesture near her during the snapping of a photo while she slept (fully clothed); and secretly squeezed a woman's buttocks (likely for a joke) during a pose with her at the Minnesota State Fair while her husband took the picture.

Consider the patterns: Roy Moore has accumulated nine independent accusers whose stories are corroborated in detail. His town knew Roy in his 30s as a pursuer, even a predator, of young girls. Donald Trump holds the current record of 17 accusers, whose accusations also are documented and corroborated. He was recorded admitting, nigh bragging, that he gropes unsuspecting women. And don't give me the "locker-room talk" defense. Like many professional male athletes and many regular men have stated, I've been in locker rooms — men don't talk like that, there or anywhere else, unless they think like that.

Al Franken has one overzealous-without-permission kissing incident in 2006 and one poor-humorous-judgment buttocks-squeezing incident in 2010. No pattern.

Two instances of poor judgment, insensitivity, boorishness, and a temporarily warped sense of humor.

But no pattern.

Sen. Franken needs to pay a price; there is no denying that. He has apologized sincerely. He's called for his own Senate ethics investigation. He might deserve to be censured. He no doubt will increase his already super-strong support of women's issues including strengthening sexual harassment policies. He should do a speaking tour or two (with all fees going to women's causes) explaining his behavior, what he's learned from it, and imploring other men to raise their consciousness about this issue.

But Al Franken should not resign or be expelled from the Senate.

Obviously this would be reevaluated if more incidents come to light. Then there would be a pattern. I'll admit it. I'll be crestfallen, dejected, despondent, hangdog, heartsick, mournful, and woebegone. But I'll admit it.

In late-breaking news, Rep. Joe Barton (R-Texas) was exposed Wednesday in a sexting scandal. Apparently Mr. Barton sent explicit nude photos and videos of himself over a three-year period to a woman he met on the internet. An unknown source publicly posted one of the most disgusting of those photos. When the relationship soured, Joe threatened the woman with retaliation if she tried to use the photos and videos to hurt his career. She recorded his threat and admission of sexual guilt on a phone call. In response to the story, Rep. Barton issued a statement saying that while separated from his wife he had "consensual ... sexual relationships with other mature adult women."

On a lighter note, even Joe Barton says Roy Moore is not fit to serve in Congress.■

11/30/17 — Traditional Thanksgiving: Turn on the Game, Please Pass the Nativism

This year's Thanksgiving get-together with my Caucasian extended family was traditional fare: we celebrated at Mom and Dad's house where I grew up; reminisced with lots of aunts, uncles, and adult nieces and nephews after the traditional feast; watched the traditional NFL Detroit Lions game on television; and traditionally avoided any discussion of politics, current events, or religion.

"How can I liven up this party?" I asked myself. "I know. I'll go out to the car and put on my new Colin Kaepernick No. 7 NFL football jersey."

I had worn it only once before then, in the company of some liberal buddies, so it hadn't had a good test run yet.

I nonchalantly re-entered my parents' house and was spotlighted right away by two 20-something nephews. I own the *away* version of the San Francisco 49ers jersey, so the bright crimson "7" and letters K-A-E-P-E-R-N-I-C-K against the brilliant white backdrop really caught their eyes. Additionally I'm a known fair-weather football fan, so I in my new jersey — any jersey — would be flagged immediately as standing out.

One of the 20-somethings, knowledgeable about all-things NFL, produced a wide smile and said, "Ohhhh Noooooo" in a friendly but chiding kind of way. The other young nephew, not a football fan, needed an explanation, which I was happy to provide. This nephew, though not a sports fan, is an open-minded thinker. After my explanation, he immediately *got* what his Uncle Tom was conveying.

Kaepernick Recap

For the uninitiated, Colin Kaepernick was the San Francisco 49ers' starting quarterback who began "taking a knee" last year during the pregame national anthem. This was in respectful protest of the statistically high number of American Black men killed by police (or neighborhood-watch guys) who have not been held accountable. You might have heard of the Black Lives Matter movement. Subsequently several other NFL players began dropping to one knee during the anthem in embrace of Kaepernick's protest. Note that Colin settled upon kneeling rather than sitting because he was advised that kneeling is seen as a more reverential, almost prayerful form of dissent.

Then President Trump began tweeting and speaking about those "son-of-a-b*tch" pro football players who should be fired for exercising their First Amendment rights (while, by the way, breaking no NFL rules). After that, the practice of taking a knee during the anthem was adopted by a multitude of players, and even some coaches and owners, for a few games. Additionally other team personnel locked arms on the sidelines and put supporting hands on kneelers' shoulders in solidarity.

Colin Kaepernick's San Francisco contract expired at the end of last season and, despite apparent early support from certain owners, no team has picked him up. Some NFL (and MAGA) apologists state that his playing abilities simply have diminished. But many independent surveys and quarterback statistical analyses have been published showing Kaepernick's skills falling somewhere in the middle of all current NFL starting quarterbacks and at the top of all backups. His lack of a contract offer clearly is a blackballing by owners to keep Colin out of the league.

I bought a Colin Kaepernick jersey because I support the protests against statistically high numbers of Black men killed by police with no accountability; I condemn President Trump's racism in attempting to shut down those protests; and I oppose the blackballing of Kaepernick.

Back to Thanksgiving

So anyway, while I was modeling my new Kaepernick jersey, one aunt said under her breath, "Well, that's not right; some of our family's veterans fought for the American flag."

After I gave the Black Lives Matter explanation to my 20-something nephew, a forty-something nephew said with a haughty look and tone — wait for it — "Well, *All* lives matter. And besides that, Blacks are killing Blacks."

What!?

In all fairness, anyone who knows me (and my extended WASP family) knows that I fully expected the *All lives matter* retort; in fact I intentionally dangled the bait. But the follow-up non sequitur from this middle-aged nephew of "Blacks are killing Blacks" threw me off a little. This is the kind of irrational connection someone like Trump would ... Ahhhhhhh.

Yes, there are Donald supporters in my extended family, though the *All-lives-matter* guy probably would say he was one of the reluctant Christian-Right Trump supporters who only are in it for the Supreme Court picks. He would say he doesn't support Donald's misogyny. And he would say Donald isn't racist.

Right.

Yeah, I let him have it. First, I addressed the non sequitur, then the sequitur: "If you're referring to *Black-on-Black crime*, there is far more white-on-white crime in this country. But the real point is, whatever statistics you might be imagining, 'Blacks are killing Blacks' has zero relationship to the statistically high number of Black men killed by cops without accountability."

Second: "The kneeling protest is not against the American flag or the national anthem or our veterans. It is a respectful protest — against the killing of Black men by police — during a moment of enhanced public attention, i.e., during the anthem. It's intended to raise consciousness about an issue that is tearing our nation apart. Therefore it is done during a national ceremonial occasion."

I stood up, did an imaginary outstretched-arm mic drop, then spiked the imaginary football before my end-zone dance *(— writer's embellishment)*.

In reality I shut up. Things got a little quiet for a while, then we all resumed nonpolitical football talk while watching the Lions lose to the Cowboys.

I left my jersey on.

Upshot

It's clear to antiracists that *All-lives-matter* Caucasians are racist to some degree, though the latter steadfastly deny it. I'll stipulate that there are gray shades of bigotry, and un-bigoted perfection does not exist. But when a white person says, "All lives matter" in response to mention of the Black Lives Matter movement, they exhibit profound ignorance of BLM's meaning. Sure, when taken out of context, *All lives matter* is a nice, though obvious (therefore in this case, meaningless) sentiment. But when it comes to *Black Lives Matter*, they're ignorant of — they *ignore* — the root of the movement: that too many Black men die at the hands of police who are not held accountable.

There is statistical evidence; there is anecdotal evidence; there is historical evidence.

The political rise of Donald Trump has given blatant racists comfort and latent racists permission to come out of the closet. Most racists, however, adamantly deny their status, often holding up their non-use of epithets. In many ways they're more harmful to society than admitted bigots. Racism is much more than epithets and slurs. Those who support discriminatory politicians and policies while simultaneously denying their inherent bigotry are committing the worst of it.

Adam Serwer (Who?)

Donald Trump is a product of underlying American racism. No writer I know of has explained this more clearly than Adam Serwer of *The Atlantic*.

> "The specific dissonance of Trumpism — advocacy for discriminatory, even cruel, policies combined with vehement denials that such policies are racially motivated — provides the emotional core of its appeal. …

> "While other factors also led to Trump's victory — the last-minute letter from former FBI Director James Comey, the sexism that rationalized supporting Trump despite his confession of sexual assault, Hillary Clinton's neglect of the Midwest — had racism been toxic to the American electorate, Trump's candidacy would not have been viable."

> (Serwer, Adam; "The Nationalist's Delusion"; *The Atlantic*; 11/20/2017.)

Serwer supports one of the theories I laid out in my book *Barack vs. the Anti-PC: Laying the Groundwork for a 2016 Donald Trump Presidential Run:* that the election of President Obama was the catalyst for a Trump rise — though Mr. Serwer was more succinct and clear than I was:

> "Birtherism is a synthesis of the prejudice toward Blacks, immigrants, and Muslims that swelled on the right during the Obama era: Obama was not merely Black but also a foreigner, not just Black and foreign but also a secret Muslim. Birtherism was not simply racism, but nationalism — a statement of values and a definition of who belongs in America. By embracing the conspiracy theory of Obama's faith and foreign birth, Trump was also endorsing a definition of being

American that excluded the first Black president. Birtherism, and then Trumpism, united all three rising strains of prejudice on the right in opposition to the man who had become the sum of their fears. … The great cataclysm in white America that led to Donald Trump was the election of Barack Obama."

(Ibid.; Serwer; 11/20/2017.)

In my book I parsed this theory with the observation that party leaders ignored vicious Republican tea party bigotry for short-term gain. GOP leadership wouldn't publicly support the perpetuation of racial epithets, dog-whistling, and conspiracy theories, but it also would not denounce it. Party bosses signaled to their base that anything goes. Donald Trump heard that message loud and clear. To its shock the Republican establishment lost control of its party and now has reaped what it has sown.

"Half a century after Senator Barry Goldwater of Arizona rose to prominence by opposing civil rights legislation designed to dismantle Jim Crow, the Republican Party's shift toward nativism foreclosed another path not just to ethnic diversity, but to the moderation and tolerance that sharing power with those unlike you requires."

(Ibid.; Serwer; 11/20/2017.)

Adam Serwer uses exit polls and other data to disprove the myth that President Trump's populist popularity was responsible for his win, that the poor, working class, and middle class of all ethnic groups thought he would raise them up economically and save them from being left behind:

"Overall, poor and working-class Americans did not support Trump; it was white Americans on all levels of the income spectrum who secured his victory. ... The answer cannot be that Black Americans were suffering less than the white working class or the poor, but [instead it's] that Trump's solutions did not appeal to people of color because they were premised on a national vision that excluded them as full citizens."

(Ibid.; Serwer; 11/20/2017.)

Finally, Mr. Serwer answers the question that perplexes all anti-Trump thinkers: Why do Donald's supporters stick with him in spite of his transparent con artistry, i.e., his pathological lying, broken promises to his base, and swamp-*filling* appointments and policies?

"One measure of the allure of Trump's white identity politics is the extent to which it has overridden other concerns as his administration has faltered. The president's supporters have stood by him even as he has evinced every quality they described as a deal-breaker under Obama. ... Conservatives portrayed Obama as a vapid celebrity; Trump *is* a vapid celebrity. ... There is virtually no personality defect that conservatives accused Obama of possessing that Trump, himself, does not actually possess."

(Ibid.; Serwer; 11/20/2017.)

Read the full article. Adam Serwer brilliantly has dissected the racist underpinnings of Donald Trump's appeal.

Now what do we do about it?

What do you call a white-guy uncle wearing his Colin Kaepernick jersey to a Caucasian family gathering to provoke middle-aged nephews and enlighten 20-something nephews?

A good start.■

"I'll say this for you. He's been one of the best presidents I've served under."

(Hatch, Orrin, R-Utah, U.S. senator; Q&A with reporters; outside Senate chambers; 11/29/2017.) *(responding to a question about President Trump and his inflammatory racist tweets earlier in the day)*

12/07/17 — Flynn Flips – and so Does Flake, Collins, McCain, and the RNC

[TOPICS: Trump-Russia; GOP tax bill]

Jeb Bush said it best and first during the Republican presidential primaries: Donald Trump is a chaos candidate and if elected will give us a chaos presidency. Who knew Jeb was clairvoyant?

Well it doesn't take a weatherman to know which candidate will be the chaos president (or which way the wind blows — *apologies to Bob Dylan).* Virtually all of the 16 or 17 other GOP primary candidates on those early debate stages knew — they *knew* — Donald Trump was a walking disaster for their party.

In my 2017 book I laid out how the Republican establishment made a deal with Beelzebub during the Obama years. It looked the other way and gave tacit approval to tea party racism, nativism, and xenophobia in return for obstructionist support. Ultimately the establishment lost control of its party. By the 2016 presidential primaries it already was too late to stop The Donald, though the GOP didn't know it at the time.

Most Democrats and many independents knew from the beginning of his candidacy that if Trump were elected president, he'd be a catastrophe for the country. In keeping with Donald's love for "mosts," he has surprised even us Never Trumpers by being the worst, most dangerous, most corrupt, most democracy-damaging president our country ever has seen. He's exceeded our wildest fears. A glance at the headlines during any given week tells the story in a nutshell. Television newsrooms across the country have gotten used to throwing out their prepared outlines because Trumpian outrages, atrocities, and attention-seeking tantrums materialize so quickly.

"This Rusher Thing" — Evidence Is Piling Up

You might have heard of "this Rusher thing, with Trump, and Russia." It's been in the news. Donald is being investigated to see if he or his campaign partnered with Vladimir Putin and buds to cheat Hillary Clinton out of the presidency. And like President Richard Nixon, he's also being investigated for possibly covering up the dirty deeds.

Unlike Nixon, Trump seems to have signaled many of his peccadilloes through public statements. He's been so brazen with these that a patina of legality lingers over the illegal acts.

> "Russia, if you're listening, I hope you're able to find the 30,000 [Hillary Clinton] emails that are missing. I think you will probably be rewarded mightily by our press."
>
> (Trump, Donald, R-N.Y., 2016 presidential candidate; news conference during [Fla.] Democratic National Convention; Doral, Fla.; 7/27/2016.)

At the time, many Democrats called this suborning espionage. GOP leaders scrambled to make sure the American people knew Republicans still viewed Russia as the bad guys.

Consider this one:

> "And in fact, when I decided to just do it [fire FBI Director James Comey], I said to myself, I said, you know, this Rusher *[sic]* thing, with Trump, and Russia, is a made-up story."
>
> (Trump, Donald, R-N.Y., U.S. president; interview conducted by Holt, Lester, *NBC News;* White House; 5/11/2017.)

At the time, many Democrats, Republicans, and legal pundits called this an admission of obstruction of justice. Until this interview, the White House's stated reasons for firing Comey were Justice Department recommendations (from the attorney general and his deputy) based on Comey's "mishandling" of the Clinton email probe.

Currently many pundits still surmise that these two public statements (and others) by the president represent 1) collusion with a foreign power to alter our election, and 2) obstruction of justice to cover up that collusion. New timeline information pertaining to the Trump campaign, transition, and presidency further backs up these hypotheses. Hidden pieces of the puzzle are uncovered almost daily through persistent investigative reporting, special counsel indictments and charges, congressional committee hearings, and presidential tweets.

Thursday

This past week alone has produced an avalanche of bad news for the president. Last Thursday it was uncovered that Trump had asked the Republican chair of the Senate Judiciary Committee to wrap up its Trump-Russia investigation quickly. After the chair responded that it will take as long as it needs to take, Donald then contacted several GOP committee members to ask *them* to pressure the chair to end the probe quickly.

Take a breath.

This development by itself would have had President Barack Obama's head on a platter instantly — and most any other president's. But President Trump, protected by congressional Republicans, continues to dodge bullets like this; and this is but one of a hail of bullets exposing Trump's criminal liability. Most Republicans in Congress have sold their souls — tacitly condoning grounds-for-impeachment misconduct — to enact their plutocratic agenda and protect their jobs.

It gets worse. Also last Thursday, Adam Schiff (D-Calif.), top Democrat on the House Intelligence Committee, reported that Attorney General Jeff Sessions declined to answer when asked in closed hearings that day, "Were you ever instructed by the president to take any action that you believed would hinder the Russia investigation." Declined to answer!

Friday

On Friday former Trump national security adviser Gen. Michael Flynn pleaded guilty to perjury concerning his false statements to the FBI. In those statements, he denied discussing sanctions relief with the Russian ambassador during the presidential transition. Note that Flynn also could be exposed to a boatload of other charges (illegally working with multiple foreign governments, conspiracy to kidnap a Turkish national, bribery, etc.) along with his son. But in return for full and complete cooperation with special counsel Robert Mueller, Flynn's sentencing is delayed, additional charges are on hold, and Flynn's son is uncharged for now.

In other words if Michael Flynn gives prosecutors everything he has on the Trump campaign, transition, and administration — having been a senior member of all three — prosecutors will wait and see about the perjury sentence and all other charges including those against the junior Flynn.

Where do you think Michael Flynn's loyalties lie now? Note that Donald has shown no loyalty to anyone he has fired, *ever*, except Flynn. On the seventh day of the Trump administration, Sally Yates, acting attorney general, informed the White House that Flynn had lied to Vice President Mike Pence and could be "compromised," i.e., blackmailed, by Russia. The president kept his national security adviser on the job a full 18 days after that. Trump only relented when *The Washington Post* broke the story of Yates' Jan. 26, 2017, White House meeting. Since then Trump has continued to praise Flynn, speculated he might have erred in firing Flynn, has railed that Flynn received unfair treatment, and privately messaged Flynn to "stay strong."

Saturday

Now it starts to get good — and all this happened in one week.

> "I had to fire Gen. Flynn because he lied to the Vice President and the FBI. He has pled guilty to those lies. It is a shame because his actions during the transition were lawful. There was nothing to hide!"
>
> (Trump, Donald, R-N.Y., U.S. president; Twitter post; 12/2/2017.)

You *know* that after the reports of Gen. Flynn flipping Friday, President Trump's lawyers demanded he not comment, anywhere, anyhow, on that development or the Russia investigation in general. Donald lasted about 24 hours. He couldn't stop himself. This represents an especially dangerous time for America. If the president can't refrain from implicating himself in a criminal conspiracy and blowing up his presidency — and he refuses to listen to any of his lawyers or advisers — what's to stop him from responding after Kim Jong Un announces: "Call me Little Rocket Man one more time, you presidential dotard, and I will launch our nukes"?

Why does the tweet about Flynn implicate the president in obstruction of justice? 1) Trump knew Flynn lied to Pence, but he was not supposed to have been aware that Flynn lied to the FBI — Sally Yates never told the White House about that; and 2) the day after *The Washington Post* story forced Trump to fire Flynn, Trump cleared the room — of his attorney general, chief of staff, and others — and spoke with FBI Director James Comey alone. According to Comey's contemporaneous memo to "the file," the president said to him, "I hope you can see your way clear to letting this go, to letting Flynn go. He is a good guy. I hope you can let this go."

OK, first, if President Trump found out that Flynn had lied to the FBI on the same day he found out Flynn had lied to VP Pence (Jan. 26, 2017), this is all the more reason to ask, Why did President

Trump keep Michael Flynn on as national security adviser, attending high-level meetings with foreign governments, 18 more days? — and fire him only after the Yates-White House meeting was outed?

Second, if Donald knew Michael Flynn had lied to the FBI when Trump met with Director Comey, then asking Comey to let the Flynn thing go seems to be a clear attempt to stop the investigation of a known crime, i.e., obstruction of justice.

To cover up knowledge Trump was not supposed to have had, the White House tried to say that just this one time — never before and never again — Trump personal Russia lawyer 76-year-old John Dowd dictated this tweet to a "staffer" who then posted it to the president's Twitter account. Literally no one believes this. In any event the tweet looks just as bad either way.

Monday

Team Trump members are defecating in their tighty-whiteys after the Flynn plea and flip. It really looks like the end is near. All along they've been maintaining there was no collusion with Russia to effect a Trump electoral win, and there has been no obstruction of justice because there is nothing to cover up.

On Monday the president's legal team members flipped their strategy. Now they've put out the word that technically there is no legal statute with the word *collusion* in it, therefore collusion is not a crime. Moreover they say the president cannot obstruct justice because as head of the entire U.S. legal system, if the president does it, it's not illegal. Even Nixon didn't say this aloud until after he was forced out of office.

First, *collusion* has been used in the media as shorthand for *conspiracy to cooperate* with a foreign government to alter a U.S. election. Clearly *that* is illegal. Michael Flynn's assurances to Russia that the Trump administration would reverse Obama's Russian sanctions (implemented upon Russia's annexation of part of Ukraine and its interference in the U.S. election) after Donald gets into office might be traitorous.

Second, reportedly almost all constitutional and legal experts say the Trump administration's new defense — that the president can't obstruct justice — is dead wrong. It's been tried before and has not worked.

Tuesday

It's Dec. 5, 2017, and the week is not over yet. Special counsel Robert Mueller has subpoenaed Donald Trump's financial records from Deutsche Bank. There are three things to know about Deutsche Bank: 1) they have been fined $400 million-plus for Russian money laundering; 2) Trump's administration has stifled a new Deutsche Bank investigation initiated by the Obama administration that could result in a fine of *billions* of dollars for additional Russian money laundering; and 3) Deutsche Bank is the only large bank in the world that has continued to loan Mr. Trump money after his large bankruptcies and large loan defaults — including defaulting on past loans from Deutsche.

Donald Trump has criminal exposure on four fronts: Russian collusion, obstruction of justice, financial corruption, and heavy conflicts of interest as president. I believe he will face reckoning on all four.

Wednesday

If it wasn't bad enough for Michael Flynn, another bombshell was revealed Dec. 6, 2017. At 12:11 p.m., Inauguration Day, 11 minutes after President Trump was sworn in, Flynn texted a former business associate from his seat at the ceremony. He told him their prospective partnership with Russian players to build nuclear power plants throughout the Middle East was "good to go" and the partners should "put things in place"; now that Trump was in office, the Russian sanctions precluding that deal would be "ripped up."

Not a good look.

Apparently the guy on the receiving end of that text told another friend he was with. That friend told authorities. The information made its way to the House Oversight Committee. The committee agreed to hold off on releasing the news — at the request of special counsel Bob Mueller — until Michael Flynn was indicted or pleaded guilty.

Who Else Flipped?

In the title of this week's article, I said that Flake, Collins, McCain, and the RNC also flipped. Let me sum up.

Early Friday morning, the same day Michael Flynn officially entered his plea agreement to cooperate with prosecutors (aka *flipping*), the Senate passed its version of the tax overhaul bill. Republicans like to say it's tax *reform*, but most of the country realizes it's a transfer of wealth to the already rich from the working poor and the U.S. debt, with no real *reform* to the process of tax collection and administration. The debt will increase by at least $1.5 trillion (over 10 years) and that's if all rosy GOP projections come to pass.

Sen. Bob Corker (R-Tenn.) was the only Republican holdout to stick to his no-debt-increase guns. Senators Jeff Flake (R-Ariz.), Susan Collins (R-Maine), and John McCain (R-Ariz.) all rolled over after previously indicating they would not vote to increase the debt. Sen. Collins also was against weakening the ACA. The Senate version of the tax bill, however, eliminates the individual mandate, one of three legs supporting the Obamacare-ACA stool (along with no preexisting conditions and providing subsidies). She flipped on that.

Sen. McCain gave an impassioned floor speech during the attempt to repeal and replace Obamacare, about how harmful it was to government for one party to shove through legislation quickly with no serious hearings and no input from the opposition party. With his decision on tax cuts for the wealthy, he flipped and voted to do exactly that.

These three senators succumbed to the belief of their leaders that any tax bill — no matter how bad — was better than not passing *something* by the end of the year. If this didn't fly, Republicans would be burdened with the fact that they went the entire first year of Trump's presidency without passing a single significant piece of legislation. They voted for a stinker bill to prop up their GOP midterm vote count in 2018. They put party over country.

Speaking of putting party over country, the Republican National Committee decided to resume supporting and funding Roy Moore's (R-Ala.) special election senatorial candidacy. This is significant because after nine women (including underage-teenagers-at-the-time) went public with accusations of sexual misconduct and assault against Mr. Moore, the RNC cut ties with his campaign. Senate Majority Leader Mitch McConnell (R-Ky.) urged Moore to drop out of the race knowing that if he did, the Democrat, Doug Jones, would be elected. McConnell was praised by members of both parties.

Many other Republican leaders unendorsed former state Supreme Court Chief Justice Roy Moore and called for his withdrawal from the election. Note that Moore already was kryptonite to many Republicans because of being twice-removed from the bench for violating the Constitution and because of his white nationalist, far-right-Christian beliefs.

A couple of weeks went by. Moore stayed in the race. The RNC wondered what got into it in the first place, flipped, and resumed supporting the many-times-alleged sexual-assaulter Republican.

If this sounds like déjà vu all over again, you're right: This is almost exactly what happened after the *Access Hollywood* tape came out exposing candidate Trump as the misogynist sexual assaulter that he is. Billy Bush was fired from *NBC* for just *listening* to Trump, while Donald went on to become president.

And the GOP is the party of child molesters, sexual predators, justice-obstructers, and colluders — and their sycophantic congressional enablers.■

Quotes of the Week

"[The Republican tax plan] is death to Democrats. [The bill will] go after state and local taxes, which weakens public employee unions. [It will] go after university endowments, and universities have become playpens of the left. And getting rid of the [individual] mandate is to eventually dismantle Obamacare."

(Moore, Stephen, Heritage Foundation member, conservative economist, tax policy adviser to Trump presidential campaign; as cited in Kapur, Sahil; "'Death to Democrats': How the GOP Tax Bill Whacks Liberal Tenets"; *Bloomberg News;* 12/5/2017.) *(saying the quiet part out loud)*

"I, of all people, am aware that there is some irony in the fact that I am leaving [office] while a man who has bragged on tape about his history of sexual assault sits in the Oval Office and a man who has repeatedly preyed on young girls campaigns for the Senate with the full support of his party."

(Franken, Al, D-Minn., U.S. senator; floor speech; 12/7/2017.) *(in his Senate resignation speech after multiple charges of sexual misconduct)*

12/14/17 — Dignity and Respect

> "'I do respect him. Well, I respect a lot of people, but that doesn't mean I'll get along with them,' Trump told [*Fox News'* Bill] O'Reilly. O'Reilly pressed on, declaring to the president that 'Putin is a killer.' Unfazed, Trump didn't back away, but rather compared Putin's reputation for extrajudicial killings with the United States. 'There are a lot of killers. We have a lot of killers,' Trump said. 'Well, you think our country is so innocent?'"
>
> (Phillip, Abby; "O'Reilly Told Trump That Putin Is a Killer. Trump's Reply: 'You Think Our Country Is so Innocent?'"; *The Washington Post*; 2/4/2017.)

As I was digesting Wednesday morning's shocking news that Doug Jones (D-Ala.) narrowly had won the special election to replace former Sen. (now U.S. Attorney General) Jeff Sessions (R-Ala.) as the junior senator from Alabama, certain public comments from recent days and earlier in the year came to mind. I present these as a microcosmic montage of where this country has been during 2017 and where I think it is going.

"You Think Our Country Is so Innocent?"

Two weeks into his presidency, Donald Trump continued defending and *respecting* Vladimir Putin. Upon hearing *Fox News* interviewer Bill O'Reilly point out that Putin is a "killer," Donald stood up for the killer, essentially telling Bill the United States is just as bad: "We have a lot of killers. Well, you think our country is so innocent?"

Whatever happened to American exceptionalism? It's still astonishing to me and many thoughtful Republicans that the vast majority of GOP voters and congressional members could tolerate this type of Russian-apologist sentimentality and the concurrent dissing of our country. Trump-mania is a form of mass hypnosis, mass hysteria that causes people to discard previous values.

The president exhibits his incompetence and depravity in many ways: Russian conspiracy and collusion; pecuniary conflicts of interest; financial corruption; obstruction of justice; racism, nativism, and xenophobia; a cornucopia of other discriminatory beliefs and policies; sexual misconduct and misogyny; nepotism resulting in unqualified advisers; spine-chilling swamp-filling appointments; dangerous narcissism; exceptionally low emotional intelligence; exceptionally low regular intelligence; unhinged temperament begetting frighteningly poor judgment; terrifying impulse control; dreadful constitutional ignorance; knuckle-headed climate change denial; embarrassing boorishness on the world stage; and more. Play along at home. Add your own reasons to call for his resignation.

I believe President Trump is going down sometime in 2018 due to one or more of the personal shortfalls mentioned previously. (I'm rooting for "pecuniary conflicts of interest." I like the sound of that one.) The following quotes buttress a roundup of reasons he must go.

"A Trumpian Buffet of Prejudices"

Former *New York Times* executive editor Howell Raines is a respected though not well-known voice on the political pundit stage. Raines' quote about the GOP candidate in Alabama's senatorial special election sums up the kindred worldviews of Mr. Trump and Mr. Moore:

> "Roy Moore [is] trying to see if that same old trick [of George Wallace bigotry] will work on the people of this

much-misserved state. ... Roy Moore is offering up a Trumpian buffet of prejudices."

(Raines, Howell, *The New York Times* former executive editor; *MSNBC's The Beat* with Ari Melber; 12/11/2017.)

If you follow politics much you probably know that President Trump wanted to endorse Roy in the Alabama senatorial special election GOP primary. But so-called establishment Republicans talked him out of it. They believed, rightly so, that Moore's white nationalist, homophobic, hyperbolic far-right-Christian views were toxic to the party. But since that's right where Trump is (though Donald's Christian angle is completely opportunistic), Moore and Trump were the real ideological brothers.

Mr. Trump was persuaded instead to support primary candidate Luther Strange, the "respectable" Republican who already was keeping the Senate seat warm between former Sen. Jeff Sessions' ascendency to U.S. attorney general and the special election.

Roy Moore beat Luther Strange in the primary by 9 points. The president was humiliated and furious. He hates to be on the losing side. And his gut had told him Moore was his guy all along.

Then nine women credibly accused Moore of sexual misconduct and child sexual molestation. Then the Republican National Committee pulled its financial support for Moore. Then Senate Majority Leader Mitch McConnell and other prominent Republicans — to their credit — told Moore to drop out of the race.

The president stayed mum. Moore refused to drop out. Republicans gradually warmed back up to Moore and the RNC resumed support.

Then President Trump went all in for the child molester because 1) if he gave an inch to Moore's accusers he would have to do more Trump-'splainin' about his own multiple accusers, and 2) he wanted to maintain the current level of GOP control of the Senate

(52-48), no matter the cost to his party, to pass something — anything.

Then Roy Moore lost to Democrat Doug Jones by 1.7%.

Alabama has not elected a Democratic senator since 1992 — and even that guy later converted to GOP-ism. The white nationalist Republicans were stunned. The thoughtful Republicans were relieved not to have the Moore albatross around their necks. Trump was furious — again. And the country was given hope that Trumpism can be defeated even in one of the reddest states in the union.

Oh, and then Trump said he knew Moore wouldn't win anyway (with an exclamation point!):

> "The reason I originally endorsed Luther Strange (and his numbers went up mightily), is that I said Roy Moore will not be able to win the General Election. I was right! Roy worked hard but the deck was stacked against him!"
>
> (Trump, Donald, R-N.Y., U.S. president; Twitter post; 12/13/2017.)

"One of Our Attorneys — Is a *Jew!*"

The day before the Alabama election, Team Moore decided they needed to push back against antisemitic accusations. Apparently Roy had slammed billionaire Democratic supporter George Soros recently, clearly implying the Jewish Soros was going to hell because of his faith:

> "His agenda is sexual in nature, his agenda is liberal and not what Americans need. It's not our American culture. Soros comes from another world that I don't identify with. No matter how much money he's got, he's still going to the same place that people who don't recognize God and morality and accept his salvation are going. And that's not a good place."

(Moore, Roy, R-Ala., U.S. senatorial candidate; interview conducted by Fischer, Bryan; *American Family Radio's The Ordinary People Society;* 12/4/2017.)

So during one of Roy's rare appearances in the campaign's final week they trotted out his wife, Kayla, to tell supporters this:

"Fake news would tell you that we don't care for Jews. I tell you all this because I've seen it all so I just want to set the record straight while they're here." *(smiles snidely and waves to the press; crowd applauds)* "One of our attorneys — is a Jew!" *(smiles very snidely; crowd titters)*

(Moore, Kayla, R-Ala., spouse of Roy [U.S. senatorial candidate]; campaign event; Midland City, Ala.; 12/11/2017.)

The performance was so laughable that many pundits suspected Roy and Kayla *knew* this would only buoy the antisemitic perception but that they didn't care. The contemptuous emphasis Kayla snarled when she said, "… is a *Jew!*" — followed by the smart-*ss smile she flashed — could only confirm to the world that, "Yes, we don't care for Jews."

This type of stunt is close to Donald's heart. Yeah, son-in-law Jared is an Orthodox Jew and daughter Ivanka converted to Judaism when she married Jared. But when the microphones and cameras are off, Trump would say, "they are two of the good ones, a credit to their race — or whatever you call Jew-ness."

"Kirsten Gillibrand Would Do Anything for Campaign Contributions"

The other day, Sen. Kirsten Gillibrand (D-N.Y.) called for President Trump's resignation over the 17 or so credible accusations of sexual misconduct and assault against Donald. The president responded:

> "Lightweight Senator Kirsten Gillibrand, a total flunky for Chuck Schumer and someone who would come to my office 'begging' for campaign contributions not so long ago (and would do anything for them), is now in the ring fighting against Trump. Very disloyal to Bill & Crooked-USED!"
>
> (Trump, Donald, R-N.Y., U.S. president; Twitter post; 12/12/2017.)

The president tweeted this on the day of the Alabama election. Some Alabamians still were deciding for whom to vote. Among those Alabamians were women. Some experts believe this tweet played a role in tilting the election for the Democrat, Jones. Exit polls showed Trump's job performance rating in the state at 48% approval, 48% disapproval. He has lost the supermajority of voters in that state who will follow him blindly.

It took eight years for most Americans to decide they like the Affordable Care Act, aka Obamacare. Interestingly the tipping point seemed to come when they were threatened with losing it. It has taken less than one year for a majority to decide they do not like Donald Trump: the man or his policies. As of Wednesday the Monmouth University Polling Institute and the Pew Research Center show the president with a 32% approval rating, the lowest for these two polls since Inauguration Day.

Poll numbers fly around like crazy, and it's always important to check sources. But the numbers representing poll questions like, "Should President Trump be impeached?" or "Should Congress investigate the accusations of Trump sexual misconduct?" or "Do you think the president is untrustworthy?" continue to rise persistently, month by month.

"Not Fit to Clean the Toilets in the Barack Obama Presidential Library"

The *USA Today* editorial side traditionally is politically neutral. It never has endorsed a political candidate and has only "non-endorsed" two in its history, one being white supremacist David Duke. This is the paper of travelers throughout airports and hotels in America. It has earned the sobriquet *McPaper* for a reason: Like McDonalds, *USA Today* maintains its national customer base by being consistently predictable, inoffensive, and noncontroversial.

But the president went a step too far for the editorial board of the periodical you find outside your Holiday Inn Express room door each weekday morning:

> "A president who would all but call Sen. Kirsten Gillibrand a whore is not fit to clean the toilets in the Barack Obama Presidential Library or to shine the shoes of George W. Bush."

> (editorial board; "Will Trump's Lows Ever Hit Rock Bottom?"; *USA Today;* 12/12/2017.)

This classic will go down in history. This is like Ronald McDonald saying, "Everybody likes a Big Mac, but presidential sexual predators like them the most." Of course if McDonalds ever dissed President Trump — a notorious consumer of two Big Macs, two Filets-o-Fish, and a large chocolate shake for dinner — its stock would fall dramatically.

"This Entire Race Has Been About Dignity and Respect"

Which brings us to Doug Jones:

> "This entire race has been about dignity and respect. This campaign has been about the rule of law. ... As Dr. King liked to quote, 'The moral arc of the universe is long but it bends toward justice.' ... You helped bend that moral arc a little closer to that justice and ... you sent it right through the heart of the great state of Alabama."
>
> (Jones, Doug, D-Ala., U.S. senator-elect; victory speech; Birmingham, Ala.; 12/12/2017.)

Even though Roy Moore lost, the GOP has been stained as the party that supports sexual assaulters, the party of Trump and Moore. Though Mr. Moore lost, it still stands that the president threw the entire weight of his office behind the Alabama Republican. Many other prominent Grand Old Party members did the same. Heck, Alabama's governor, Kay Ivey, said she believed Roy Moore's accusers but *still* was voting for him. At least Donald hid behind his smug, phony belief that Moore's weak denials were exculpatory.

One of the reddest of red states, Alabama, has decided that "dignity and respect" trump blind party loyalty.

I like it: "dignity and respect." ∎

12/21/17 — Politicos of the Lie

"**P**oliticos of the Lie." This article's title is a play on M. Scott Peck's important 1983 book, *People of the Lie*. For those unsure of the word, *politico* simply refers to a politician and, loosely, to one who works in the business of politics. (Hey, I had to look it up somewhere along the line, too.) I could have titled it "Apparatchiks of the Lie," but it didn't have the same ring.

You might know Peck, a psychiatrist, from his more famous books in *The Road Less Traveled* series. In *People of the Lie* he lays out his findings, as a psychotherapist, about the basis of evil in certain persons and how it is manifested in pathological self-serving duplicity and narcissism.

> "Another reaction that the evil frequently engender in us [is] confusion. ... Lies confuse. The evil are 'the people of the lie,' deceiving others as they also build layer upon layer of self-deception. ...

> "It is necessary that we first draw the distinction between evil and ordinary sin. It is not their sins per se that characterize evil people, rather it is the subtlety and persistency and consistency of their sins. This is because the central defect of the evil is not the sin but the refusal to acknowledge it ... their *absolute* refusal to tolerate the sense of their own sinfulness. ...

> "A predominant characteristic ... is scapegoating. Because in their hearts they consider themselves above reproach, they must lash out at anyone who does reproach them. ... Scapegoating works through a mechanism psychiatrists call projection. ... When they are in conflict with the world, they will

invariably perceive the conflict as the world's fault ... They *project* their own evil onto the world."

> (Peck, M. Scott, MD; *People of the Lie: The Hope for Healing Human Evil;* 1983.)

Sound like any politico you know? Donald Trump is the epitome of these three characteristics: 1) he lies to confuse the electorate; 2) he refuses to acknowledge any mistake or sin no matter how small; and 3) he scapegoats through projection, so transparent even his followers see through it but they don't care.

Now I know what you're thinking: All politicians lie. Yes, all politicians likely have lied at some time in their careers just as all of us likely have sinned at some time in our lives. But the key factor here as Peck points out is the "persistency and consistency" of the lies and the refusal to acknowledge them.

Barack

His political opponents love to declare that President Obama was a liar. Consider one of their prime examples:

> "If you like your health care plan, you keep your health care plan."

> (Obama, Barack, D-Ill., U.S. president; town hall meeting; Central High School, Grand Junction, Colo. [and many other instances]; 8/15/2009.) *(referring to the Affordable Care Act, aka Obamacare)*

I laid out my response to this accusation in a previous article. Here are the highlights. Obama was not lying. At worst he made a mistake. Furthermore he only was half-wrong. His mistake was not accounting for normal turnover. A new job certainly could bring a new insurer and different eligible providers. President Obama was half-right in that so-called grandfathered plans and their existing policyholders did not have to change anything.

Barack Obama ultimately acknowledged his promise went too far. In a Nov. 7, 2013, *NBC News* interview he offered this apology: "I am sorry that [many Americans] are finding themselves in this situation based on assurances they got from me. ... We're going to do everything we can [for] folks ... in a tough position as a consequence of this."

There are many more false accusations from the right about Barack Obama lies. To be fair, he did tell a few as president. *The New York Times* has compiled a comprehensive listing of President Trump's and President Obama's lies while in office. They determined that Obama averaged about two falsehoods per year. (Leonhardt, David & Philbrick, Ian P. & Thompson, Stuart A.; "Trump's Lies vs. Obama's"; *The New York Times;* 12/14/2017.)

Republicans, however, have made an art form of lying to confuse, mislead, and bamboozle the voting public.

Newt

Many experts trace the modern-age roots of blatant, pernicious Republican lying to the rise of Newt Gingrich (R-Ga.) and his engineering of the 1994 GOP takeover of the House of Representatives. Gingrich was the prototype that paved the way for a Trump presidency.

Newt was the serial philanderer who lambasted Democrats for philandering. Newt was a loud voice for repealing Obamacare (solely because of its eponymic nature) and its individual mandate after arguing *for* a form of the mandate just a few years earlier. And Newt denied climate change was anthropogenic (caused by humans) in time for his 2012 presidential run, after jointly pleading in a public service announcement with Rep. Nancy Pelosi (D-Calif.) for all Americans to help fight (human-produced) global warming.

"As The New Republic observed in a recent analysis, Gingrich is one of the inventors of the GOP right wing's current style of 'say-anything politics,' in which both facts and principle are subordinate to short-term expediency. This is, in short, the politics of the big lie."

(White, Jack; "Why Newt Gingrich Is Beyond Satire";
The Root; 12/9/2011.)

Newt is credited with helping to kill comradery between congressional opponents. You've heard the stories of back when congressional members of opposing parties used to play tennis together and attend each other's family picnics? Speaker of the House Gingrich discouraged that. He preferred his members to cut social contacts with the other team. It was much easier to lie about them that way — you didn't have to face them afterward.

Newt Gingrich popularized the demonization of opponents instead of respectful disagreement:

"[Democratic policies would bring to America] the joys of Soviet-style brutality and the murder of women and children."

(Gingrich, Newt, R-Ga., U.S. representative; floor speech; 1983.)

"People like me are what stand between us and Auschwitz."

(Gingrich, Newt, R-Ga., U.S. representative; as cited in Cummings, Jeanne; "Gingrich out to Save America"; *Atlanta Journal-Constitution;* 1/16/1994.)

"There is a gay and secular fascism in this country that wants to impose its will on the rest of us, is prepared to use violence, to use harassment. I think it is prepared to use the government if it can get control of it. I think that it is a very dangerous threat to anybody who believes in traditional religion."

(Gingrich, Newt, R-Ga., former U.S. House speaker; *Fox News' The O'Reilly Factor;* 11/14/2008.)

"I am convinced that if we do not decisively win the struggle over the nature of America, by the time [my grandchildren] are my age, they will be in a secular atheist country, potentially one dominated by radical Islamists and with no understanding of what it once meant to be an American."

(Gingrich, Newt, R-Ga., 2012 presidential primary candidate, former U.S. House speaker; campaign speech; Cornerstone Church, San Antonio, Texas; 3/27/2011.)

Newt has carried on his efforts through the current day. Not surprisingly he's one of President Trump's greatest champions.

Mitt

After Mitt Romney (R-Mass.) clinched the Republican presidential nomination for president in late May 2012, it was just him and incumbent president Barack Obama left to duke it out. Mitt also had pursued the nomination in 2008 but lost to Sen. John McCain (R-Ariz.). Romney, though not as blatantly as Newt Gingrich, carved out a long-term solid reputation as an equivocating flip-flopper, another form of GOP "say-anything" politics.

Consider these comments from his fellow Republicans:

"I don't know how to respond to some of [Gov. Romney's] attacks] because his position may change tomorrow."

(McCain, John, R-Ariz., U.S. senator, 2008 presidential primary candidate; post-campaign event news conference; Burlington, Iowa; 12/28/2007.)

"[Mitt Romney is] making up things. ... I don't know, maybe you have another word for it. The only word I know in Arkansas, we kind of kept it simple there: We called it dishonest."

(Huckabee, Mike, R-Ark., 2008 presidential primary candidate, conservative writer and *Fox News* commentator, former governor, ordained Southern Baptist minister; campaign event; Iowa; 12/29/2007.)

"He spent more time on the road to Damascus than a Syrian camel driver."

(Huckabee, Mike, R-Ark., conservative writer and *Fox News* commentator, 2008 presidential primary candidate, former governor, ordained Southern Baptist minister; *Do the Right Thing;* 2008.) *(referring to Mitt Romney's numerous policy "conversions" on the road to the 2008 presidential election)*

"[Mitt Romney is] assuming that the American people are stupid. ... Someone [like Romney] who will lie to you to get to be president, will lie to you when he is president."

(Gingrich, Newt, R-Ga., 2012 presidential primary candidate, former U.S. House speaker; post-campaign event news conference; 1/1/2012.) *(the pot calling the kettle a pot)*

"I think that the notion that Mitt Romney has been on both sides of many issues is not a surprise anymore to anyone in the country, whether you are Republican, Democrat, Indiana Independent. I think it's baked into the cake at this point."

(Schmidt, Steve, R-N.J., 2008 McCain-Palin presidential campaign chief strategist; *MSNBC;* 10/17/2012.)

With members of the same party like these, Who needs enemies? Even *Newt Gingrich* says Romney is a serial liar.

To no one's surprise, Donald Trump endorsed Mitt Romney for president. This was during the height of Trump's birtherism campaign promoting the lie that Barack Obama was a Muslim born in Kenya. To his credit, Romney (almost) never repeated those lies. To his shame, Romney also never repudiated those who promoted the lie, when so many of his supporters were cheering on Trump's thinly veiled racist conspiratorial fairy tale.

Donald (and His Tax "Reform" Bill)

Yesterday the House and Senate passed President Trump's long-awaited tax bill. Donald will sign it soon. Embedded in this bill is a pack of some of the biggest, boldest lies ever told by a president and his Republican congressional leaders.

There has been much written about the falsehoods used to sell this bill to the American people and a few recalcitrant Republican senators. Not a single Democratic legislator bit — not out of obstructionism but out of a genuine moral concern for the country. Democrats voted against their personal interests to protect the people. The biggest story surrounding this bill is how well known the lies are about it. Polls indicate people think it's bad for the country by a 2:1 ratio. Here are the lowlighted mendacifications:

The tax cuts are aimed primarily toward the middle class. They are not. They're aimed primarily at the rich and corporations. Here's the statistic you need to know: 83% of the tax-cut benefits go to the top

1% of the income spectrum. Many experts estimate 9% of middle-class families will see a tax *increase* immediately. All will see an increase eventually because the business tax cuts are permanent but the middle class tax cuts expire.

The tax cuts will pay for themselves. They will not. They're projected to add $1.5 trillion to the national debt over 10 years. The vast majority of economists agree that any GDP growth or tax revenue increases barely will dent this debt increase. Moreover historically, supply-side (trickle-down) economics never has worked.

The bill reforms the tax code. It does not. There never was any serious attempt to simplify. Most individuals' taxes likely will be *more* complicated. Whatever happened to filing our taxes on a postcard?

Sen. Susan Collins (R-Maine) cares about the debt and the ACA. She does not. She allowed herself to be manipulated into a horse trade for her vote but got no horse in the deal. The ACA's individual mandate is eliminated with no offsetting fix. This means 13 million people could be thrown off health care coverage, and everyone else will see their premiums rise by 10%. At the last minute, Collins knew she had been double-crossed by Senate Majority Leader Mitch McConnell (R-Ky.) but she voted for the bill anyway. Conservative columnist Jennifer Rubin says, "It is hard to think of a lawmaker whose reputation has been harmed more than hers." Although Bob Corker has to be running a close second.

Sen. Bob Corker (R-Tenn.) cares about the debt. He does not. After stating for months that he wouldn't vote for any bill that raises the debt "by even one penny," at the last minute he went along to get along — plus at the last minute they threw in a real estate provision that will give him (and Donald) a boatload *more* money in tax savings.

Tax cuts will create new jobs and raise wages. They won't. Most economists agree that corporations currently are sitting on record amounts of money. If they were going to raise wages and expand they would have done so already. Ultimately corporations will reward executives and buy back their stock with the extra money.

The tax bill will cost President Trump a lot of money. It does the opposite. He claims to be working for the people against his own financial interests. But anyone who reads the bill's highlights can see he'll come out hundreds of millions of dollars ahead.

President Trump pledged to eliminate the carried-interest loophole (which benefits rich hedge fund managers and participants). This was a public relations lie. It never came up in negotiations surrounding the bill.

Congressional Republicans were under pressure to please their rich-people donor base or risk losing their rich-people support. Oops, that one is true.

> "The infuriating part of this is that none of the snake-oil salesmanship, the debt creation, the procedural sleights of hands, the heightened income inequality, the secret deals, and the contempt for voters was necessary. A revenue-neutral corporate tax reform coupled with a payroll tax break for middle- and lower-income Americans was entirely possible — with wide bipartisan support. But that was not what Republicans, their donors, and the fleet of lobbyists wanted."

> (Rubin, Jennifer, conservative opinion writer; "The Most Infuriating Falsehoods About the Tax Bill and Those Who Told Them"; *The Washington Post;* 12/18/2017.)

All 48 Democratic caucus senators, including the three richest senators overall, voted against their own interests for the good of the country and the people. This one is true.

Donald's Orwellian Strategy

Donald Trump is the biggest *Politico of the Lie* in many generations. He's taken Newt Gingrich's say-anything brand of Republican politics to dizzying heights, "the likes of which this nation has never seen before."

Like Gingrich and Romney, Trump is a skillful flip-flopper. He ensures that his support base always will be able to agree with *one* of his positions on an issue and repress the others.

He lies to confuse the electorate. He knows that muddying the waters is a powerful tool to fool the vast pool of people who do not obsess over fact-checking.

He refuses to acknowledge any mistake or sin no matter how small. His supporters see this as strength though critically thoughtful people realize it's a colossal weakness. Still, it's great for water-muddying.

He scapegoats through projection, so transparent even his followers see through it. But they don't care. Again, they see strength as in he's a "counterpuncher" who fights back. Yes, he fights back against reality. It's become a given that whatever President trump criticizes or attacks, he, himself, is guilty of.

The overwhelming reality is that Donald Trump has made lying acceptable, normal. He's desensitized the people to prevarication and mendacity. And he's given all his supporters including Republicans in Congress permission to lie as well, also with apparent impunity.

Look at the GOP's false selling points for the tax bill. Look at the meetings with Russians. Look at *Fox News:* calling special counsel Bob Mueller's Russia probe "a coup in America"; calling the FBI a "KGB-type operation." Look at Trump's seven forbidden words for the CDC (*vulnerable, entitlement, diversity, transgender, fetus, evidence-based,* and *science-based*). Look at Donald dropping climate change from the U.S. list of global threats, and eliminating that topic from the EPA website. Look at his false promises to Kentucky that he'll bring back coal. Look at his laughable false promises to drain the swamp.

Look at Vice President Mike Pence's obsequious, mendacious, pabulum-filled tribute to the president at yesterday's Cabinet meeting. No kidding: It sounded like a North Korean general's tribute to Dear Leader. Then Dear Leader spoke and every word out of President Trump's mouth was part of a perjurious stream of self-serving, self-adoring bull feces.

Truth is the foundation of everything. Without it we are lost. We don't demand perfection. Barack Obama averaged about two falsities per year of his presidency. And when he realized his errors, he generally stopped repeating them. By the same metric, Donald Trump has told about 124 blatant lies in his first year as president:

> "Trump is different. When he is caught lying, he will often try to discredit people telling the truth, be they judges, scientists, FBI or CIA officials, journalists, or members of Congress. Trump is trying to make truth irrelevant. It is extremely damaging to democracy, and it's not an accident. It's core to his political strategy."
>
> (Leonhardt, David & Philbrick, Ian P. & Thompson, Stuart A.; "Trump's Lies vs. Obama's"; *The New York Times*; 12/14/2017.)

Per M. Scott Peck, "Lies confuse. The evil are 'the people of the lie,' deceiving others as they also build layer upon layer of self-deception." This is one of the reasons we've never seen con artistry like Donald Trump's. He's learned to sell his own fiction until he believes it.

It's authoritarian. It's Orwellian. ∎

12/28/17 — Revisiting George Orwell in the New Year

> "Totalitarianism demands, in fact, the continuous alteration of the past, and in the long run probably demands a disbelief in the very existence of objective truth."

> (Orwell, George, author [*Animal Farm, 1984*]; *Books v. Cigarettes* [essay]; 1946.)

No, I'm not saying Donald Trump's administration has reached totalitarian proportions. I *am* saying he grasped a long time ago these two integral epistemological components of totalitarianism. And he's employing them now to the fullest extent he can.

Totalitarianism, and its little brother authoritarianism, are not established overnight. They're borne of a few cancerous cells ultimately resulting in a full-blown oncological state.

I doubt Trump ever seriously has studied either of these *-isms*. Most likely Donald is a perfect alignment of events and personal characteristics coming together in his life: 1) he was born into a fabulously rich family who provided business loans and a limitless financial safety net; 2) he never had to answer to anyone in childhood or adulthood except his father; 3) he developed a pathologically narcissistic worldview with an addictive need for attention and praise; and 4) he developed a superb confidence artist's grasp of shamelessly defining his own "truth."

Credit Where Credit Is Due

In the general election, Donald benefitted from another set of perfect-alignment components: the GOP's long-term, absurd vitriolic hatred of strong Democratic woman Hillary Clinton; proved pro-

Trump Russian election interference; and FBI Director James Comey's questionable judgment in press-conferencing his qualified exculpation at the end of the Hillary-email investigation (July 2016), then mistakenly publicly reopening the probe 11 days before Election Day, in late October.

President Trump also benefitted from that strange American political animal, the Electoral College, which gave him the presidency in spite of a record 2.86 million *more* votes cast for his opponent.

It is true, however, that when Trump blew through the Republican primaries and vanquished 16 or 17 strong GOP candidates, he did this on his own, deserving all the credit. Donald Trump exploited the skills he had learned in the business and celebrity worlds — con artistry, bluster, bloviation, bullying, rewriting his past, creating his own reality, successfully rewriting anyone else's past who crossed him — to crush his primary opponents psychologically then electorally.

Now he approaches his one-year anniversary in office. He's reversed most previous accomplishments with the name Barack Obama attached to them, hurting millions of people in the process simply out of spite. He's violated the separation between White House and Department of Justice. He has appointed Cabinet secretaries to emasculate the departments they head. He's consistently blown away the norms and traditions that hold our American form of democracy together. He continues to try to govern the United States in the same authoritarian manner he exercises with the Trump Organization.

The president likely has financial corruption to account for. He has mob connections to explain. He likely has committed illegal conspiracy to effect his election. He likely has obstructed the process of justice in myriad ways, some publicly. Vladimir Putin likely has pressured him into submission with visions of golden-shower videos dancing in his head. Donald divides us. He insults us. He discriminates against us.

Yet he holds 40% or so of us in his autocratic gaze, in a kind of mass hypnosis.

The Good Fight

Over the past couple of weeks, I've participated in an online political discussion group that is approximately 90% pro-Trump. I bait participants into "debate" with liberal article posts and comments. Most of them hurl vile one-liners at me.

I did get into a long thread with a pseudo-intellectual Donald supporter, Joey, who thought he could throw lots of insignificant facts and figures against the wall in support of his arguments. I pointed out how Joey feigns intellectualism by creating an avalanche of self-important-sounding drivel, which serves only to obfuscate the point at hand. I threw his insignificant facts and figures back at him and beat him up badly, dissecting his logical fallacies mercilessly.

We exchanged crossfire and witty retorts for an hour. I thought Joey would never give up. Finally he accused me of evading the subject and not answering his debate questions, called me ignorant, and said my attitude was "unattractive."

I posted, "Ad hominem attacks: the last refuge of the uninformed."

He made one last gasp, replying that I was the uninformed one throwing "ad homs" around.

I posted, "Projection: the last refuge of those who won't admit their ad hominem attacks."

Joey never responded. He went down for the count and I got the knockout.

Pyrrhic Victory

I clearly won the battle of wits and witty retorts with Joey and his vituperative cohorts. But it was a Pyrrhic victory. I was depressed about it for a few days. Why? There are a few reasons I've come up with. First, throughout my rough-and-tumble back and forth with these Trump group members, I have to admit I did throw a few "ad homs" myself. In fairness to me, there were some twisted trolls in there spewing some of the worst virulence you can imagine. But afterward I felt soiled by joining in, even if it was self-defense.

Second, though I generally came out on top (at least in my own mind) when reason and logic were involved, their dismissal of truth and reality was upsetting, disturbing. Remember the two components of totalitarianism in the Orwell quote at the beginning of this article: "continuous alteration of the past" and "disbelief in the existence of objective truth." They believe without reservation all of Donald's alterations of the past as he rewrites his first year in office. And frighteningly, they believe in Trump's concept of *fake news*, the disbelief of objective truth. They repeat the phrase constantly.

There essentially are two types of Trump supporters in that group: abusive trolls and pseudo-intellectual snobs. "And some, I assume, are good people" *(— thanks to Donald Trump).*

The members of this group automatically disbelieve any objective information if it comes from *The New York Times* or *The Washington Post.* Trump hasn't just convinced them that the editorials are wrong. He's convinced them that no objective information these newspapers report can be believed — because they report the truth about Donald and his behavior. Note that the *Post* and *Times* never hesitated to report into the ground every detail about Hillary's emails or (husband of top Hillary aide) Anthony Weiner's sexual offenses.

The group members extend this powerful false concept of *fake news* to any media outlet that reports anything negative about Trump and Trumpism no matter how objectively and accurately they report it.

A real danger is that Trump supporters have been trained to disbelieve professional journalism even when it isn't reporting on Trump. It's similar to the damage Donald does as he bashes the FBI because they're closing in on him. When he says the FBI's reputation is "in tatters" and the bureau is "tainted," Trump doesn't care that this hurts the FBI's ability to do all of its other, non-Trump work.

Andrés Miguel Rondón

For the time being I've resolved not to engage directly with Trump disciples. It's too depressing, frustrating, and exhausting. When someone does not care about objective truth, there is, rhetorically, nowhere to go. So what are the reasonable, fact-respecting two-thirds of the electorate supposed to do?

First, resolve to support special counsel Robert Mueller's investigation to the fullest. Be ready to take to the streets if Trump interferes. In a way, we're fortunate the president has criminal legal exposure on so many fronts: conspiracy with a foreign government to alter the election; obstruction of justice; financial conflicts of interest; and general corruption. If *all* he did was lie pathologically to the electorate, we'd be stuck with him through 2020.

Second, I believe Andrés Miguel Rondón lays out a good alternative line of defense. Rondón is a Venezuelan citizen, born and raised there, who saw the rise and fall (death) of Hugo Chávez, "who ruled as precisely the sort of faux-populist strongman that Trump now loves to praise."

Ultimately Rondón says we must find a way to create a better message than President Trump's. Additionally we must stop arguing with his hardcore supporters, trying to prove them wrong, and belittling them. We are their enemy and our opposition only fuels their stubborn denial of facts and their confirmation bias, and strengthens Donald's emotional hold on them.

The Problem:

> "Trump [populism] did all of the above — constructing an alternate reality that gave his supporters a concise answer to their question[, Why, after so many years of work, am I still suffering?], and the hope of a solution. It doesn't matter that it's all bogus. To Trump voters, a fake reality — especially

one laden with obvious enemies and golden promises — is better than nothing, or more of the same. …

"Like religion, populism asks for blind allegiance, dismisses truth as the unconditional value of meaning, and arises from a certain unverified, mythological coherence. And like religion, populism promises a distant resolution — one that never comes, of course, but is constantly dangled in front of its supporters, who are soothed by the expectation. …

"Constantly trying to disprove, on a daily basis, what Trump says will only bait people into their confirmation biases. It will increasingly entrench moderates on both sides unto abstention or, worse, the extremes. What you need is a powerful message with which to substitute a true plan for a false spell."

> (Rondón, Andrés Miguel; "Donald Trump's Fictional America"; *Politico*; 4/2/2017.)

The Solution:

"If you want to fight Trump effectively, you have to learn to think like they do and give up altogether the prospect that scandal will one day undo him. … As long as Trump is still swinging back, scandals help him to polarize the country further. The scorn of his adversaries, in the eyes of his supporters, proves that he's doing exactly what they voted for him to do: dismantling a rigged system that they believe destroyed their hopes. …

"It does not matter that he is eroding the nation's democratic institutions. That this combat is dangerous, hypocritical, built on lies. That you, after all, are innocent. His supporters are convinced that you are to blame. Until you can convince them otherwise, they will cheer him on. The name of the game is polarization, and the rookie mistake is to forget you are the enemy."

(Rondón, Andrés Miguel; "To Beat President Trump, You Have to Learn to Think Like His Supporters"; *The Washington Post*; 12/26/2017.)

Oh, and reread George Orwell's *Animal Farm*. I know you slogged through it in high school. But it takes on a whole 'nother meaning in the wake of President Trump's first year in office.■

01/04/18 — Jerry Springer: Presidential Edition

[TOPICS: new book out, "Fire and Fury" by Michael Wolff]

> "Regarding the president's tweeting habits, I haven't been a fan until this week. I'm warming up to the tweets."
>
> (McConnell, Mitch, R-Ky., U.S. Senate majority leader; news conference; Washington, D.C.; 12/22/2017.)

President Donald Trump is about the one politician who can make Mitch McConnell seem a little less nauseating.

Mitch made this cerebral quip at a news conference days after the House and Senate passed the GOP tax plan. The implication was that Donald mostly had stayed on message (read: stayed out of the way) with his tweets and other public statements leading up to the bill's final passage. Also the president hasn't dissed Mitch in about a month.

The colossal McConnellean hypocrisy in even this mildly humorous sound bite screams at us: As long as Donald doesn't hurt Mitch's feelings, the Senate majority leader is OK with the president spewing childish sobriquets at other leaders in this country and around the world. This is like Ralphie saying as long as Scut Farkus doesn't beat him up this week, who cares what the bully does to Flick, Schwartz, or even his own little brother, Randy (a little *A Christmas Story* reference).

The president is an immature train wreck. As sick as we get of reading about his latest transgressions, we must not take them for granted, rolling our eyes and complaining, "Well, that's just Trump." He *wants* to desensitize Americans to his dangerous idiocy, for many reasons. His primary reason is that he believes these distractions will save him from the special counsel Russia investigation. Though it's not good for our personal short-term health, the long-term health of American democracy depends upon all of us maintaining our outrage.

Trump Doctrine

Let me stop myself right here. Everyone with a brain knew Donald Trump was the most vile, egomaniacal confidence artist ever to befoul a television screen. After one year in office, we also know that his cyclopean ignorance, astronomic narcissism, and galactic immaturity are dangerous enough to threaten Armageddon *(— thanks to Merriam-Webster for the Brobdingnagian intensifiers).*

I was going to review Donald's outrageous Twitter posts since the beginning of the new year: you know — the ones that look like a C-student fifth grader conducting foreign policy. He tweet-insulted Pakistan. He tweet-insulted Iran. But I'm tired of rehashing President Trump's latest outrages. Well, maybe just one today. He tweet-threatened Kim Jong Un:

> "North Korean Leader Kim Jong Un just stated that the 'Nuclear Button is on his desk at all times.' Will someone from his depleted and food starved regime please inform him that I too have a Nuclear Button, but it is a much bigger & more powerful one than his, and my Button works!"
>
> (Trump, Donald, R-N.Y., U.S. president; Twitter post; 1/3/2018.)

The Trump Doctrine finally has been defined: "Mine is bigger than yours."

One more on domestic policy?

"Crooked Hillary Clinton's top aid, Huma Abedin, has been accused of disregarding basic security protocols. She put Classified Passwords into the hands of foreign agents. Remember sailors pictures on submarine? Jail! Deep State Justice Dept must finally act? Also on Comey & others"

(Trump, Donald, R-N.Y., U.S. president; Twitter post; 1/2/2018.)

If you can't get enough of these New Year's tweets, see *The New York Times* article "Trump's First Big Twitter Day of 2018: Analyzing Nuclear Buttons and the 'Corrupt Media'" (Jan. 3, 2018).

Breaking News

I'm looking at my computer and this story is breaking: *The Guardian* has obtained a prerelease copy of Michael Wolff's book *Fire and Fury: Inside the Trump White House*, to be dropped Jan. 9, 2018. Now *New York* magazine has just posted a long article by Mr. Wolff based on his book.

Wolff somehow tagged along with the Trump transition team, then camped out in the West Wing from Inauguration Day through October 2017, most of Donald's first year in office. During and after that time he conducted hundreds of interviews with current and former White House principals and underlings. There were apparently no ground rules placed upon his access and he made no promises as to content. This is extremely un-Trumpian considering we know Donald requires legally airtight nondisclosure agreements with even the McDonald's delivery crew.

Michael Wolff's book has exploded on the news landscape this week. Everyone will be reading this thing. Between former top aide Steve Bannon's declaration of war on Trump World and all the insider dirt and unfiltered comments, this book could be a massive blow to Donald's presidency, second only to special counsel Bob Mueller's ultimate collection of indictments and plea deals. The mistake by the president in allowing Mr. Wolff nearly unlimited access to the White House serves as a microcosm for the entire Trump transition and presidency.

On June 9, 2016, the infamous Trump Tower meeting took place that included Don Jr., Paul Manafort, Jared Kushner, and Russian operatives claiming to have dirt on Hillary Clinton. Mr. Wolff reports that Steve Bannon described this meeting during the campaign as "treasonous" and "unpatriotic."

> "Even if you thought that this was not treasonous, or unpatriotic, or bad sh*t, and I happen to think it's all of that, you should have called the FBI immediately. … [Furthermore,] the chance that Don Jr. did not walk these jumos up to his father's office on the twenty-sixth floor is zero. …

> "They're going to crack Don Jr. like an egg on national TV. … You realize where this is going. This is all about money laundering. Mueller chose [senior prosecutor Andrew] Weissmann first and he is a money-laundering guy. Their path to f***ing Trump goes right through Paul Manafort, Don Jr., and Jared Kushner … It's as plain as a hair on your face. … It goes through Deutsche Bank and all the Kushner sh*t. The Kushner sh*t is greasy. They're going to go right through that. They're going to roll those two guys up and say play me or trade me."

> (Bannon, Steve, former [Trump] White House senior political strategist; as cited in Wolff, Michael; *Fire and Fury: Inside the Trump White House;* 2018; as cited in Smith, David; "Trump Tower Meeting With Russians 'Treasonous,' Bannon Says in Explosive Book"; *The Guardian;* 1/3/2018.)

For the record, Steve Bannon hates Jared Kushner. And he's not big on Don Jr. either. Here's the president's response after the excerpts broke:

> "Steve Bannon has nothing to do with me or my presidency. When he was fired, he not only lost his job, he lost his mind. … Steve doesn't represent my base; he's only in it for himself. … Steve pretends to be at war with the media, which he calls the opposition party, yet he spent his time at the White House leaking false information to the media to make himself seem far more important than he was. It is the only thing he does well. Steve was rarely in a one-on-one meeting with me and only pretends to have had influence to fool a few people with no access and no clue, whom he helped write phony books."
>
> (Trump, Donald, R-N.Y., U.S. president; written statement; as cited in Sullivan, Eileen & Baker, Peter; "Trump Says Bannon Has 'Lost His Mind' After Bannon Insults Donald Trump Jr."; *The New York Times;* 1/3/2018.)

And just for good measure:

> "Trump is not spared [in the book]. Wolff writes that Thomas Barrack Jr., a billionaire who is one of the president's oldest associates, allegedly told a friend: '[Trump's] not only crazy, he's stupid.' Barrack denied that to *The New York Times.*"
>
> (Smith, David; "Trump Tower Meeting With Russians 'Treasonous,' Bannon Says in Explosive Book"; *The Guardian;* 1/3/2018.)

According to this book, almost every middle- to upper-level White House player has damning things to say about colleagues and President Trump. Almost all of Trump's aides are quoted as using some synonym of the word *idiot* to describe the president. And Donald at one time or another has called most of his staff members idiots.

Add to this the earlier reports of Secretary of State Rex Tillerson calling Trump a "f***ing moron"; national security adviser H. R. McMaster calling Donald a "dope" and an "idiot," with the intelligence of a "kindergartner"; chief of staff Gen. John Kelly hanging his head in shameful disgust behind the dais while Donald makes another embarrassing speech; and First Daughter Ivanka regularly lampooning her father's Just for Men orange-blond comb-over (as Wolff recounts); and you've got the ultimate reality show.

This is *Jerry Springer: Presidential Edition*.

Now You Tell Me

The *New York* magazine article focuses on the overriding concept that no one in the Trump campaign thought he would win, and few in the campaign *wanted* him to win. They were all — including Donald — sure he would lose and were counting on it. And they were all — excluding Donald — probably sure he *shouldn't* be president.

In the weeks before the election, Mr. Trump already was planning to leverage his increased celebrity, floating rumors about a Donald Trump media network. Third campaign head Kellyanne Conway would be an on-air political pundit star. Ivanka would go out into the world with a freshly burnished retail brand. Jarvanka (Steve Bannon's portmanteau-alicious slur for the team of Jared Kushner and his wife, Ivanka) would be American royalty. Donald Jr. would revive the Brylcreem hair-care brand.

They all viewed this sure-to-lose presidential run as a spectacular springboard for the rest of their careers. It would be (increased) fame and fortune for everyone. The losing election campaign would be the most successful *marketing* campaign ever devised.

"This is bigger than I ever dreamed of," Wolff reports Trump telling Roger Ailes a week before Election Day. "I don't think about losing, because it isn't losing. We've totally won."

When the shocking win materialized late into election night, Don Jr. said his father looked as if he had seen a ghost. Melania cried. In a bad way. According to Wolff, Donald previously had assured her he never would be president.

In the coming weeks, high jinks ensued:

> "From the moment of victory, the Trump administration became a looking-glass presidency: Every inverse assumption about how to assemble and run a White House was enacted and compounded, many times over. The decisions that Trump and his top advisers made in those first few months — from the slapdash transition to the disarray in the West Wing — set the stage for the chaos and dysfunction that have persisted throughout his first year in office. This was a real-life version of Mel Brooks' *The Producers*, where the mistaken outcome trusted by everyone in Trump's inner circle — that they would lose the election — wound up exposing them for who they really were."

> (Wolff, Michael; "Donald Trump Didn't Want to Be President"; *New York*; 1/3/2018.)

This explains so much. Everyone knew the Trump campaign didn't *expect* to win. But who knew they didn't *want* to win — including the candidate. That's why they totally were unprepared. As Michael Wolff tells it, however, it took President-elect Donald Trump a very short time to transition from excrement-filled Fruit of the Looms to thinking he could do the job better than anyone else.

Russia Probe

It appears Steve Bannon was in a position to understand the Russian dirt without soiling himself. He's so sure of his cleanliness that he doesn't plan to hire an attorney to guide him through the special counsel probe. Bannon, the first White House insider to volunteer damaging dirt about Trump World's alleged illegal dealings with Russia, sees the downfall coming much the same way independent legal pundits do: Don Jr. "cracking like an egg" and the money laundering going right through Paul Manafort and Jared Kushner on the path to Trump. (Of course the Michael Flynn flip also will be key.)

Mr. Wolff elaborates on this in his book: Donald Trump and the rest of the Keystone Cops did not bother covering their tracks very well because they never expected to win the presidency and be subject to the accompanying scrutiny. Then he won. What's he gonna do? Say, "No thanks"? (Although I remember scattered speculation about some version of "No thanks" at the time.) Wolff relates a conversation between then-high-level campaign adviser Gen. Michael Flynn and friends who suggested he shouldn't have accepted that $45,000 for the speech in Putin's Russia. "Well, it would only be a problem if we won," Flynn responded.

We know Trump Org. has a large web of financial transactions with Russia going back many years. Don Jr. said as much at a real estate conference in 2008: "Russians make up a pretty disproportionate cross-section of a lot of our assets. We see a lot of money pouring in from Russia." In 2013 brother Eric responded to golf writer James Dodson's question about the source of funding for Trump courses: "Well, we don't rely on American banks. We have all the funding we need out of Russia."

You know they both caught hell at home for these slips of honesty.

We know that Donald is well known for cutting legal corners and pushing the boundaries of tax law. *Fire and Fury* — with its salacious gossip, backbiting, and score-settling — is notable also for all that it corroborates about Trump's ignorance, likely Russian collusion and conspiracy, and financial improprieties. I believe 2018 is the year the Trump presidency dies.

In another deep dig at the president's Russia problem, Wolff reports that Bannon said, "If [Trump] fires Mueller, it just brings the impeachment quicker. Why not, let's do it. Let's get it on."

Otherwise, as he said on *Breitbart News Tonight* late Wednesday after the book excerpts were released and the feces hit the fan, Steve Bannon still thinks President Trump is "a great man," and he supports the president "day in and day out."

Indeed. "Let's get it on." ■

01/11/18 — Republicans Complicit

In case you've been isolated in the "sh*thole countries" of "Tann-ZANE-ee-yah" or "Nambia" *(— thanks to Donald Trump)* since New Year's Day, a book came out: Michael Wolff's *Fire and Fury: Inside the Trump White House.* It does not flatter President Trump. Some key words and phrases that have emanated from extensive White House staff interviews describing the chief executive are "childlike," "semi-literate," "mentally unstable," "idiot," "he's lost it," and others. The book is the talk of Washington, D.C., and cable news. You should check it out.

Funny thing. The White House does not like this book.

The president tweeted his defense:

> "Actually, throughout my life, my two greatest assets have been mental stability and being, like, really smart. ... I went from VERY successful businessman, to top T.V. Star ... to President of the United States (on my first try). I think that would qualify as not smart, but genius ... and a very stable genius at that!"

> (Trump, Donald, R-N.Y., U.S. president; Twitter post; 1/6/2018.)

I've often said Mr. Trump speaks like a 15-year-old Valley girl. He overuses the word *like* just as today's teenage Valley girl descendants do. In fairness, even the most stable of us geniuses occasionally let slip a "like" for filler in everyday speech. Donald's mind, however, loves the word so much that he literally *wrote in* the "like" (never mind the adolescent overuse of exclamation points).

I won't bore you with the myriad defenses of Donald's smartness by members of his team. But Nikki Haley's sycophantic comments warrant pushback:

> "Was he unstable when he passed the tax reform? Was he unstable when we finally hit back at Syria and said no more chemical weapons? Was he unstable when we finally put North Korea on notice? Was he unstable when he said, wait, we need to look at Iran because this is getting to be a dangerous situation? Was he unstable with the jobs or the economy or the stock market?"
>
> (Haley, Nikki, R-S.C., U.S. ambassador to U.N., former governor; *ABC's This Week* with George Stephanopoulos; 1/7/2018.)

Nobody said Donald is unstable all the time. His close advisers occasionally are successful at containing (read: babysitting) him and keeping the president quiet while cooler, more stable geniuses prevail. Then they let him take the credit afterward. With tax reform, he stayed out of the way as exhorted to so the GOP Congress could ram their bill through and embolden his harmful, thinly disguised plutocratic policies. With Syria, his do-the-opposite-of-Obama mentality for once fit with his generals' judgment. With "jobs or the economy or the stock market," again all he had to do was stay out of the way and not rain on the strong six-year upward economic trends he inherited from his predecessor.

With "when we finally put North Korea on notice," yes, the president was unstable. He used dangerous adolescent tweets, empty threats, and personal insults to conduct extremely sensitive foreign policy. With "we need to look at Iran because this is getting to be a dangerous situation," yes, the president was unstable. He continues to play political football with this issue, threatening to renege on a finely tuned agreement to prevent nuclear proliferation simply because the name *Obama* is connected to it.

Listen to the *BBC World Service* for an hour, respectable news and commentary from outside America: President Trump is embarrassing the U.S., scaring our allies, emboldening dictators, endangering our troops stationed in dangerous countries, and undermining our WMD bargaining power with North Korea. If you were Kim Jong Un (or a former Trump casino contractor), Would you trust Donald to keep his side of a nuclear bargain?

Republicans Complicit

The more unstable President Trump gets, the more traditional Republicans like Lindsey Graham and Paul Ryan cover for him. They are complicit in his precarious, frightening leadership. That's because most of them are selfishly myopic. As one cable pundit explained, each faction is getting what it wants from Trump. And each one is willing to overlook likely criminal activity, national security lapses, and foreign interference in American elections to get more of what it wants.

The *White Lives Matter* crowd has a close ally in the president and his bigoted policies and sensibilities. The hard-line immigration wing is getting the expulsion of Haitians, Mexicans, and Salvadorans and thinks it is getting its wall. Both those contingents are getting presidential disparagement of Haitians and Africans as coming from "sh*thole countries."

Donald's ultra-rich peers and Republican megadonors are getting their lopsided tax breaks. House Speaker Paul Ryan and tea party refugees still hope to eviscerate Obamacare, Medicare, and Medicaid. Ryan is willing to prostitute himself thoroughly for his hopes of creating an Ayn Randian utopia.

The GOP is getting what it wants, so ix-nay on the ussia-Ray obe-pray.

Many people have compared Russia-gate to Watergate. It is an apt comparison though even Watergate didn't involve conspiracy with a foreign government to commit treason (in this case, during a 21st century cyberwar). The point is that both scandals entail(ed) widespread involvement of a GOP presidential campaign and administration. Why does this tend to happen more with Republicans?

Sure, Democratic President Bill Clinton had his sexual harassment and illicit affairs scandals. As harmful as these were to the women involved and to the country's psyche, however, they were an issue of one man's personal shortcomings — for which a GOP Congress impeached him. Note that the Monica Lewinsky opprobrium originated with the Whitewater real estate investigation. Bill did lie about the women, but special prosecutor Ken Starr never found any wrongdoing in Clinton's business or presidential behavior — other than that Monica thing.

Selfish Political Ideology

So why *are* Republicans more likely to be involved in an administration-wide scandal? Because at its core, modern-day Republicanism is a selfish political ideology. Among other pillars, the Democratic philosophy is built on providing a safety net for disadvantaged Americans, especially children. The GOP can argue about whether lesser-off adults are deserving of government help. But the children have no say in their situation. If we want those kids to break the cycle and grow up to be law-abiding, productive citizens, they need Head Start programs, pre-K, school-lunch programs, child care for working-poor parents, and health care insurance. They need a leg up.

The wealthy, the large business owners and investors who have benefitted from American infrastructure, compound interest, and a silver-spoon birth have an obligation to give back through a progressive tax system, to help people at the other end of the economic spectrum. Many of the super-rich like Bill Gates and Warren Buffett get this. The Trumps of the world do not.

Republicans as a group have narrow-minded views on this subject. From early in their lives, most of them always knew they could get an emergency loan from Mom and Dad. They always knew they could get bail money and a lawyer if they made a bad decision. They knew their parents would provide a temporary roof over their heads if they needed it. They could get a cavity fixed if they were short on funds. And they knew they could take some calculated risks in life like starting a business or attending college because they had family to fall back on if necessary.

Democrats of means also know these things. But Republicans take these benefits for granted, rarely considering the people, especially the children and young people, who aren't so fortunate. They are empathically challenged as a voting bloc.

Millions of citizens do not have a safety net. Many don't have a parent in a position to help them if they lose a job, have a run-in with the law, or can't afford food or health care for their kids. Many of them don't have a parent. As the analogy goes, life is a race but not everyone is born at the front of the pack. Or try this one from George Orwell's *Animal Farm:* "All animals are equal, but some animals are [born] more equal than others."

Here's the point: Democrats' understanding of the need for a social safety net requires altruism and empathy. I'm talking as a group now: We all know individual stingy Democrats and generous Republicans. But as a voting bloc, Democrats know helping poor families, especially the children, is good for society and good for our souls. We want to give those kids born at the back of the pack a leg up.

This is why Republicans are more prone to Watergates and Russia-gates. Scandals like these involve a groupthink fed by tendencies toward selfishness (along with Newt Gingrich-like exaggerated animosity toward opponents and a high level of comfort with disinformation and untruths). Again, Bill did lie about sex with Monica. And Monica unquestionably was a victim who suffered from involvement in that whole mess. But Clinton's entire administration didn't participate in widespread crimes and the cover-up of those crimes.

Republican/Democrat vs. Conservative/Liberal

Today's Democrat, for all her party's faults, embraces a culture of life, that is, embraces a continuous moral support for equality, diversity, fairness, truth, the earth, the worker, the (biblical) stranger, freedom of (any) religion or no religion, a cultural safety net, voting rights, and an ethical government that works for the people.

Republicans love to say things like, "The Republican Party is the party of Lincoln, and the Democratic Party fostered slavery and the KKK in the past." Those things are true. But party identification is ephemeral. Liberal and conservative philosophies are consistent and that's what matters.

I am a liberal. Had I lived in Lincoln's time I would have been a *Republican* rabidly supporting abolition. Mitch McConnell, Kevin McCarthy, and Donald Trump, "conservatives," would have been *Democrats* fighting Lincoln and supporting "states' rights," supporting their right to own other human beings. I fiercely would have opposed Lincoln's second-term vice president (compromise candidate, half of the "National Union" ticket, then president), *Democrat* Andrew Johnson, whose corruption was manifest in his entrenched racism, sabotage of Reconstruction, tacit approval of the KKK, and opposition to citizenship for former slaves.

If I'd been alive during *Democratic* President Andrew Jackson's day, I, as a liberal, would have been a supporter of the *Whig* or *Anti-Jacksonian Party* vehemently opposing his Indian relocation policies, phony populism, and autocratic attempts to expand executive power. Mitch McConnell, Kevin McCarthy, and Donald Trump, "conservatives," would have been Jackson enthusiasts. This is why President Trump took the unusual step of placing a portrait of (Democrat) Andrew Jackson in the Oval Office.

And during the 1960s, I would have been a Democrat supporting the work of two presidential champions of civil rights, John F. Kennedy and Lyndon B. Johnson — but *not* supporting the racist ideology of Southern Democrats, aka "Dixiecrats."

Throughout history I might have been a Republican, Democrat, Whig, or some independent combination, depending upon the decade. But I always would have been a liberal as I am today — embracing continuous moral support for equality, diversity, truth, the earth, the worker, the (biblical) stranger, freedom of (any) religion or no religion, a cultural safety net, voting rights, and an ethical government that works for the people.

Today Republicans are light-years of morality and integrity *away* from where they were in Lincoln's time. And today the liberals are Democrats.

Go, special counsel Bob Mueller.■

01/18/18 — Republican Diaspora

For all the discussion of Republicans complicit in the evils of Donald Trump's policies, it's important to note those who have spoken out against the president's atrocities and about his unfitness for office. They're either fleeing or being pushed out of the party's new Trumpian mainstream. These members of the Republican diaspora have been willing to risk a lot. Those holding office are risking any future elected or appointed positions within the party. The rich non-officeholders are risking their country club status.

Those conservative pundits, think-tank notables, and former high-level staffers critical of Donald risk being frozen out of mainstream GOP information flow and Washington dinner party invitations, as well as incurring presidential tweet-attacks. It's easy for Democrats and independents to forget how strong Mr. Trump's party support is. We're used to hearing about the president's sturdy base of 40% or so. But the mystifying statistic is that his backing of self-identified Republicans remains in the 80s to 90s.

There will be tomes written about how Donald held onto as much support as he has, with no one reason explaining it. His clearly racist, anti-immigration principles attract a large number of loyal supporters, though it's difficult to measure specifically because there are so many shades. There are the obvious racists and xenophobes — the white nationalists. There are the in-the-closet bigots who latch onto Mr. Trump's dog-whistling and policies that thinly disguise the president's intentions — the *White Lives Matter* crowd. And there are those who blindly go along with their tribe or don't admit their bigotry to themselves — the *All Lives Matter* crowd. The total of these groups accounts for a huge bite of that 80-90%.

We have the white evangelicals who've taken rationalization to dizzying heights. They now support the most immoral person elected president since at least abolition. They don't see or care that

Trump opportunistically glommed onto their pet issues just in time to launch his campaign. They only care about opposition to pro-choice and gay rights policies, "religious (i.e., Christian) freedom," and the newly appointed judges who will support those views. They overlook the racism. They have agreed tacitly to accept the rampant adultery, sexual harassment, adult-film actor and prostitute dalliances, and admissions of sexual assault. They've laughably defended Mrs. Trump's soft-porn nude photos as akin to biblical examples of nature's beauty, and compared Roy Moore (Trump's candidate for Alabama senator) and his dating and assaulting of minor teenage girls to Jesus' stepfather, Joseph.

Then you have the so-called small-government conservatives. These are people like House Speaker Paul Ryan, the House Freedom Caucus, and even "traditional" Republicans who push through trillion-dollar-plus tax cuts for the rich (disguised as tax reform and middle-class tax relief). Then they tell us the national debt is too high so we must cut "entitlements" such as Medicare, Medicaid, the Affordable Care Act, Children's Health Insurance Program, unemployment insurance, and the Salvation Army soup line. (I might have exaggerated that last point.)

Essentially they believe in cutting revenues (taxes, etc.) to force the cutting of government services. They do this with little concern for any social safety net that, as I said last week, the wealthy and corporations should be obligated to support because of the benefits they've garnered through American infrastructure, compound interest, and silver-spoon births. They also want to cut government research and regulatory administration, which protect citizens from poisonous food and medicine, suicide-trap cars, contaminated drinking water, unbreathable air, and an ozone layerless atmosphere. To them these are pesky job-killing (read: profit-trimming) regulations.

The upshot is that all the different far-right factions get what they want from Trump as long as they ignore his attacks on American democracy, which they're perfectly willing to do.

Elected Officials

The number of GOP legislators who have decided not to seek reelection in 2018 is up to about 37 and rising. They all have their individual reasons, but we can surmise the majority don't believe they can win either their primary or general. Of that group, I believe some made the noble calculation that they could have won but only if they were willing to prostitute their principles and cozy up to President Trump — which they chose not to do.

Consider the sentiments of one in the latter category, Sen. Jeff Flake (R-Ariz.):

> "'The enemy of the people,' was what the president of the United States called the free press in 2017.
>
> "Mr. President, it is a testament to the condition of our democracy that our own president uses words infamously spoken by Josef Stalin to describe his enemies. It bears noting that so fraught with malice was the phrase 'enemy of the people,' that even Nikita Khrushchev forbade its use, telling the Soviet Communist Party that the phrase had been introduced by Stalin for the purpose of 'annihilating such individuals' who disagreed with the supreme leader.
>
> "This alone should be a source of great shame for us in this body, especially for those of us in the president's party, for they are shameful, repulsive statements. And, of course, the president has it precisely backward — despotism is the enemy of the people. The free press is the despot's enemy, which makes the free press the guardian of democracy. When a figure in power reflexively calls any press that doesn't suit him 'fake news,' it is that person who should be the figure of suspicion, not the press."

(Flake, Jeff, R-Ariz., U.S. senator; floor speech; 1/17/2018.)

Sen. Flake has been the most vociferous Republican critic of the president in Congress. You might remember his Senate floor speech last October announcing his decision not to seek reelection because he didn't feel there was a place for traditional conservatives like him in today's (Trump's) Republican Party. In that speech, Flake said he "will not be complicit" in allowing the president to compromise "American values" and "moral authority," and that the president has caused an "alarming and dangerous state of affairs." Mr. Flake also released a book last year, *Conscience of a Conservative*, in which he was highly critical of the president.

So good for Jeff. Among current and former GOP officeholders, he's spoken the most and loudest about the damage Donald is doing to American democracy. But some critics say he could and should have done more. Political integrity often is relative.

In his book, Sen. Flake chastised pre-candidate Trump for his birther initiative. Flake also claimed to have "done enough" at the time in speaking up about Donald's thinly disguised racist lies. I'm sorry, Sen. Flake. I don't remember you speaking up very loudly. If you had, you would have been a household name back then because almost no Republicans spoke up. I'm sorry: You did not do enough to disavow the Trumpian birther conspiracy while it was in progress.

The big problem for GOP members during the 2012 election cycle (when Sen. Flake won his seat) was that many were on board with Trump's evil fairy tale. But even the "respectable" ones — who knew the conspiracy story was a lie — would not denounce Trump or repudiate the falsehoods. They tried to straddle the fence with their silence. They chose not to speak out, which would have alienated the true birther believers. Simultaneously this allowed them to pander to reasonable Republicans and swing voters by not vocalizing support for the crackpot theories. In the end, they gave tacit approval to the campaign of lies. And they lost control of their party.

GOP Anti-Trumpers Could Do More

The other thing you could do right now, Sen. Flake, is call for President Trump's resignation, or call for his impeachment. The same goes for other anti-Trumpers, e.g., Sen. Bob Corker (R-Tenn.) (who also has chosen not to run for reelection), Sen. Ben Sasse (R-Neb.), 2012 GOP presidential candidate Mitt Romney, and Gov. John Kasich (R-Ohio), all of whom publicly have questioned the president's fitness for office.

If you guys really believe your party is in free fall and the president is a danger to the country, go all the way: Call on him to resign. Call on your party to begin the impeachment process. Take a *real* risk. Sure, the success of these actions is a long shot right now but the act of taking them is imperative. It has to start with a prominent Republican somewhere, just as Sen. Edward Brooke (R-Mass.) was the first Republican legislator to call for President Richard Nixon's resignation in November 1973, nine months before increasing party pressure ultimately forced it.

Other notable GOP legislators who have expressed discomfort with President Trump at one time or another are Rep. Charlie Dent (R-Pa.) and Sen. John McCain (R-Ariz.). Honorable mentions include Senators Lindsey Graham (R-S.C.) and Dean Heller (R-Neb.).

Yes, it's slim pickings. And even the heartiest of congressional Republican Trump opponents are not always consistent in their opposition to the president. They sometimes have used him or capitulated to him if their interests called for it.

But relatively speaking, Democrats and independents must support the GOP anti-Trumpers. This batch of unevenly brave Republicans is all we have in office right now. And we must reinforce the good behavior. If your dog doesn't come right away when you call, you don't scold him when he finally gets there. If you do, he's less likely to come next time — 'cause he's learned a scolding is waiting for him. You praise old Fido even if he comes late, which makes him more likely to call for the president's resignation next time.

Free Press

George Will, Jennifer Rubin, Charlie Sykes, Steve Schmidt. These are prominent anti-Trump conservative pundit members of the Republican diaspora. (Will and Sykes officially have left the GOP to become "independent conservatives.") They all believe Donald is grossly unfit for the presidency. They'll be important drivers of any successful effort to rid our government of President Trump and reunite their party. To their credit, they publicly acknowledge the dangerous governing philosophies, methods, and incompetency of the Trump presidency even without the specter of criminal behavior that special counsel Bob Mueller is likely to turn up.

Hats off to non-officeholder GOP luminaries such as Max Boot (former Romney adviser and Sr. Fellow at the Council on Foreign Relations), Evan McMullin (former CIA operations officer, former chief adviser to the House Republican Conference and House Committee on Foreign Affairs, Independent 2016 presidential candidate), and David Frum (former George W. Bush speechwriter and senior editor at *The Atlantic*). Unequivocal conservative anti-Trump voices like these are integral to the cause.

Tons of credit also must go to the dedicated investigative reporters. It's not just *The Washington Post*, *The New York Times,* and a few other print outlets anymore. The internet has its pros and cons. But a major pro is the birth of many legitimate digital media publications with their own investigative reporting staffs.

Breaking News

Stormy Daniels, the adult-film actor with whom Mr. Trump had an affair during his second year of marriage to Melania while son Barron still was breastfeeding, has written a 5,500-word exposé about sex with The Donald. The article ran in *InTouch* magazine.

Like I said: Thank God for new media and more hard-hitting reporting.◼

———————

213

My Free Gift for You

Download for FREE: *My Election 2008 Email Wars: Disinformation Before Social Media Ubiquity*

Join my email newsletter and get this e-book about conspiracy theories at the voter level before social media was a thing. This book can be downloaded to your computer and read there or transferred to any e-reader.

Download this e-book for free today at:

https://graniteword.com/free-book-my-election-2008-email-wars-2020/

The Author

Tom Ersin holds an advanced degree from Trump University, having risen to its most enlightened (and expensive) Operating Thetan Levels. No, wait — that's his Scientology training. Common mix-up. All seriousness aside, Ersin is a Macomb County, Michigan, long-time political observer, communications professional, and editor of online magazine *GraniteWord*. He's written a half-dozen non-fiction books on 21st century U.S. politics. His turn-ons are running his dog, Bob Barker, and railing about the lack of critical thinking. Find out more at GraniteWord.com. Email him at tom@graniteword.com.

~~~

Please Make This Author Happy

I hope you enjoyed reading this book as much as I did writing it. I'd be forever appreciative if you would post a review on Amazon. Just a sentence or two and a rating would be great. Reviews are lifeblood for authors and they help readers find my books.

(https://www.amazon.com/dp/B0CJXGRXL2)

Thanks a lot,
Tom
~~~

This Series

This is the second in my subseries comprising the three books:

> *Trumpism: Why Traditional Republicans Should Withdraw Support [2017-2021: A Primer]*

> *Trump's First Year in Office: The Awakening*

> *Trump's Last Year in Office: Two Impeachments and 400,000 Funerals*

All three books listed above are carve-outs from my exhaustive 1,400-page history:

> *Trump's Presidency: A Real-Time Commentative History [2017-2019]*

> *Trump's Presidency: A Real-Time Commentative History [2019-2021]*

This book, *Trump's First Year in Office: The Awakening,* is the second volume in the subseries, all drawn from the perspective of a long-time avid political observer. Think of the histories as an in-depth every-Thursday recap of all the news you were too busy to consume because you had a life and didn't realize the gravity of the dysfunction and disinformation. When you see my opinion you'll know it. Much more often, when you see facts, quotations, and details, I'm assuring you that I've backed up their accuracy with careful research and citation.

Milestones in the Trump Presidential Era

06/16/15 – ELECTION 2016: Donald **Trump announces candidacy**

07/mid/15 – GRU (RUSSIAN MILITARY INTELLIGENCE) GAINS ACCESS TO DNC COMPUTER NETWORK: **maintains access until at least June 2016**, when hacking plot was reported

05/03/16 – ELECTION 2016: Donald **Trump clinches Republican nomination**

06/09/16 – MEETING BETWEEN TRUMP CAMPAIGN, RUSSIANS: **Trump Tower meeting**, including Donald Trump Jr., Jared Kushner, Paul Manafort, Russian lawyer Natalia Veselnitskaya, et al. *(prompted by offer of "dirt on Hillary" from Russia)*

06/14/16 – 1ST REPORT OF HACKERS ACCESSING DNC SERVERS: next day, computer security firm **CrowdStrike identifies Russia as perpetrator**

07/05/16 – HILLARY CLINTON STATE DEPT. EMAIL CONTROVERSY: FBI Director James **Comey publicly closes Clinton (misuse of State Dept.) email investigation** with no charges; states Clinton team was "extremely careless" but not criminal

07/22/16 – WIKILEAKS' 1ST RELEASE OF (20,000) DNC, HILLARY CLINTON CAMPAIGN EMAILS: ultimately it would **release more than 44,000 emails, 17,000 attachments**

07/25/16 – RUSSIA ELECTION INTERFERENCE INVESTI-GATION: **FBI publicly confirms opening investigation into hacking of DNC** *(4 days later, DCCC announces it has been hacked)*

07/31/16 – TRUMP-RUSSIA INVESTIGATION BEGINS: **FBI secretly initiates counterintelligence investigation, regarding possible Trump campaign collusion with Russia**, after learning Trump aide George Papadopoulos bragged to an Australian diplo-mat, *before* WikiLeaks' surprise DNC email dump, that Russians had obtained Clinton campaign "dirt": "thousands of emails" *(this and other evidence suggested to FBI that Trump could be a witting or unwitting Russian asset; also, NYT reports Trump Campaign Chair Paul Manafort's "business dealings with prominent Ukrainian and Russian tycoons")*

10/28/16 – HILLARY CLINTON STATE DEPT. EMAIL CONTROVERSY: FBI Director James **Comey publicly reopens Clinton (misuse of State Dept.) email investigation** based on new emails found on Clinton aide's laptop

11/06/16 – HILLARY CLINTON STATE DEPT. EMAIL CONTROVERSY: FBI Director James **Comey publicly re-closes Clinton (misuse of State Dept.) email investigation**; states FBI's original conclusions have not changed

11/08/16 – ELECTION DAY: **Donald Trump defeats Hillary Clinton**; Trump wins Electoral College 306-232; Clinton wins pop-ular vote 65.9M-63.0M, 48.2%-46.1%

11/9/16 – 1/19/17 – FLURRY OF CONTACTS BETWEEN RUSSIANS, TRUMP TRANSITION TEAM: including presump-tive national security adviser Gen. Michael **Flynn asking Russian ambassador not to retaliate** over President Obama's sanctions, **assuring him Trump will lift sanctions** after inauguration; Putin obliges

01/20/17 – INAUGURATION DAY: Donald **Trump takes office** as 45th president

01/27/17 – MUSLIM TRAVEL BAN: **instituted by Trump administration, causes chaos** due to total lack of warning to, coordination with airlines and government agencies involved *(blocked by several courts, eventually superseded by other executive orders)*

01/31/17 – SUPREME COURT: President **Trump nominates Neil Gorsuch,** Trump's 1st nominee *(after Senate Majority Leader Mitch McConnell, R-Ky., had denied President Barack Obama's nominee a hearing to fill March 2016 opening)*

02/13/17 – TRUMP FORCED TO FIRE NATIONAL SECURITY ADVISER: **president fires Gen. Michael Flynn** after 22 days in office, only upon public reporting that DOJ warned White House much earlier that Flynn was security risk *(Flynn lied to FBI, denied discussions with Russian ambassador during transition, to lift Russian sanctions after inauguration)*

02/14/17 – TRUMP MEETS PRIVATELY WITH FBI DIRECTOR JAMES COMEY: **president asks Comey to stop investigation of Gen. Michael Flynn:** "I hope you can see your way clear to letting this go, to letting Flynn go." *(Comey did not agree to comply)*

04/10/17 – SUPREME COURT: **Senate confirms Neil Gorsuch,** Trump's 1st justice

05/09/17 – TRUMP FIRES FBI DIRECTOR: **president fires James Comey,** ostensibly for mishandling of Clinton email investigation; 2 days later, Trump discloses to *NBC*'s Lester Holt, "When I decided [to fire Comey], I said to myself, I said, 'You know, this Russia thing with Trump and Russia is a made up story.'"

05/17/17 – TRUMP-RUSSIA INVESTIGATION — SPECIAL COUNSEL APPOINTED: Trump's firing of FBI director prompts **appointment of Robert Mueller as special counsel** to investigate 1) Russian 2016 U.S. election interference, 2) possible Trump campaign conspiracy with Russia to help elect Trump, and 3) Trump obstruction of justice to block FBI investigation of these issues *(appointed by Deputy Attorney General Rod Rosenstein because Attorney General Jeff Sessions had recused himself from all-things Russia due to his false statements during his confirmation hearings)*

07/08/17 – TRUMP-RUSSIA INVESTIGATION: President **Trump dictates statement in Don Jr.'s name covering up real reason** (which was to collect dirt on Hillary Clinton) **for June 9, 2016, Trump Tower meeting between Trump campaign and Russians**

08/11-12/17 – UNITE THE RIGHT RALLY: **Charlottesville, Va.; large white supremacist rally** protesting removal of Gen. Robert E. Lee statue and other Confederate monuments; included infamous Tiki-torch marchers chanting, "Jews will not replace us!" *(a neo-Nazi protester intentionally rammed his car into group of counterprotesters, killing 1, injuring 35; Trump later said there are "very fine people on both sides")*

08/late/17 – HURRICANE HARVEY: affected Texas, La; Category 4, sustained winds of 130 mph, 100-plus deaths, $125B damage

09/early/17 – HURRICANE IRMA: affected northeastern Caribbean including Puerto Rico; Category 5, sustained winds of 180 mph, 80-plus deaths, $77B damage

09/late/17 – HURRICANE MARIA: affected northeastern Caribbean including Puerto Rico; Category 5, sustained winds of 175 mph, 3000-plus deaths, $90B damage

10/01/17 – MASS SHOOTING: **Paradise**, Nev., outside Mandalay Bay resort and casino on Las Vegas Strip, Route 91 Harvest outdoor country music festival; shooter: Stephen Craig Paddock, 64, Caucasian American terrorist *(60 killed, 867 injured)*

10/31/17 – TRUCK ATTACK: **New York**, N.Y., Hudson River Park bike path; driver: Sayfullo Habibullaevich Saipov, 29, Uzbekistani jihadist terrorist *(8 killed, 11 injured)*

11/02/17 – ASIA TOUR: President Trump leaves for **12-day tour** of Asian countries

11/05/17 – MASS SHOOTING: **Sutherland Springs**, Texas, First Baptist Church; shooter: Devin Patrick Kelley, 26, Caucasian American terrorist *(26 killed, 22 injured)*

11/07/17 – OFF-YEAR ELECTIONS: **Democratic wave** *(Democrats, diversity enjoy many big wins)*

12/08/17 – TRUMP-RUSSIA INVESTIGATION: **Michael Flynn**, former Trump national security adviser and top campaign aide **pleads guilty** to lying about Russian contacts before inauguration *(enters into plea agreement [flips] with special prosecutor Robert Mueller)*

12/12/17 – ALA. SPECIAL ELECTION FOR U.S. SENATE: long shot **Doug Jones (D) beats former Ala. Supreme Court Chief Justice Roy Moore (R)** by 1.7% *(Jones replaces former Sen., now U.S. Attorney General, Jeff Sessions [R] to be 1st Democratic Ala. senator since 1997)*

01/02/18 – AL FRANKEN (D-MINN.): **resigns Senate seat** *(due to sexual misconduct allegations)*

02/14/18 – MASS SHOOTING: **Parkland**, Fla., Marjory Stoneman Douglas High School; shooter: Nikolas Cruz, 19, Caucasian American white supremacist terrorist *(17 killed, 17 injured)*

04/mid/18 – MIGRANT CHILD SEPARATION: Trump administration **begins "zero tolerance" policy for illegal immigration** at southern border; policy discontinued in June after national outrage *(5,400 children separated from families for weeks, months, with no communication, in subhuman conditions; hundreds never were reunited due to administration incompetence) (2017 pilot program ultimately revealed)*

05/18/18 – MASS SHOOTING: **Santa Fe**, Texas, Santa Fe High School; shooter: Dimitrios Pagourtzis, 17, Greek American terrorist *(10 killed, 13 injured)*

06/18/18 – TRUMP-KIM SUMMIT: **Sentosa, Singapore**; 1st-ever meeting between U.S.-North Korean leaders; near-meaningless milquetoast joint statement signed *(Trump highly criticized for giving parity to Kim Jong Un on world stage with no preconditions; Trump falsely boasted that "nuclear threat has ended")*

07/09/18 – SUPREME COURT: President **Trump nominates Brett Kavanaugh**, Trump's 2nd nominee *(after "swing-vote" Justice Anthony Kennedy announced his retirement effective July 31, 2018)*

07/11-12/18 – NATO SUMMIT: **Brussels, Belgium**; Trump embarrasses self, U.S. by disrupting proceedings, chastising other members *(many prominent Americans slam Trump's behavior)*

07/16/18 – TRUMP-PUTIN SUMMIT: **Helsinki, Finland**; Trump embarrasses self, U.S. by accepting Putin's 2016 election-interference denials over U.S. intelligence *(many prominent Republicans slam Trump's statements, several invoke the word "traitorous")*

08/25/18 – SEN. JOHN MCCAIN (R-ARIZ.) DIES: succumbs to brain cancer at 81; **McCain chastises Trump** with posthumous statement *(and disinvites Trump to funeral)*

09/27/18 – SUPREME COURT: Brett **Kavanaugh Senate confirmation hearings reopened specially for Christine Blasey Ford** to testify (extremely credibly) about alleged Kavanaugh drunken attempted rape of her while teenagers; Kavanaugh also testified, rebutting the allegations in emotional, combative, mendacious, highly partisan performance

10/02/18 – TRUMP FINANCES EXPOSED: *The New York Times* prints 14,000-word article exposing **Trump's tax fraud, inheritance theft, and self-made-man myth** *(Trump calls NYT "enemy of the people")*

10/02/18 – JAMAL KHASHOGGI MURDERED: Saudi expatriate and dissident, U.S. resident, and *The Washington Post* journalist was **tortured, strangled, and dismembered** in Istanbul, Turkey, Saudi embassy by Crown Prince Mohammed bin Salman-ordered hit squad *(Khashoggi's Apple Watch recorded entire event; Trump refused to hold Saudis accountable)*

10/06/18 – SUPREME COURT: **Senate confirms Brett Kavanaugh**, Trump's 2nd justice

10/27/18 – MASS SHOOTING: **Pittsburgh**, Pa., Tree of Life synagogue; shooter: Robert Gregory Bowers, 46, Caucasian American white supremacist terrorist *(11 killed, 6 injured)*

11/06/18 – MIDTERM ELECTIONS: **Democrats take House** in landslide, pick up 41 seats, win by record-setting national generic margin of 8.6%; Republicans retain Senate, pick up 2 seats

11/07/18 – MASS SHOOTING: **Thousand Oaks**, Calif., Border-line Bar and Grill college country-western bar; shooter: David Long, 28, Caucasian American terrorist *(13 killed, 1 injured)*

11/30/18 – FORMER PRESIDENT GEORGE H. W. BUSH (R-TEXAS) DIES: at 94; **Trump attends funeral** with all former living presidents (Obama, George W. Bush, Clinton, Carter) *(but clearly stands as an uncomfortable outsider)*

12/22/18 – GOVERNMENT (TRUMP) SHUTDOWN BEGINS: **Trump shuts down government for a record 35 days** after reneging on promise to sign border security bill without border wall funding *(he reneged after conservative pundits criticized him for "giving in to the Democrats"; ultimately Trump got nothing, but caved to national pressure)*

02/14/19 – NEW ATTORNEY GENERAL: **William Barr confirmed by Senate, takes office**; Barr was appointed by Trump after sending unsolicited memo to DOJ criticizing the special counsel Trump-Russia investigation *(Barr also served as attorney general under President George H. W. Bush in early 1990s)*

02/27/19 – MICHAEL COHEN TESTIFIES: Trump former personal lawyer-"fixer" **testifies (this time truthfully) before Congress** *(exposes Trump hush-money payoffs to paramours, tax fraud, etc.)*

03/15/19 – MASS SHOOTING: **Christchurch**, New Zealand, two neighboring mosques; shooter: Brenton Harrison Tarrant, 28, Caucasian Australian white supremacist terrorist *(51 killed, 40 injured)*

03/22/19 – TRUMP-RUSSIA INVESTIGATION: **Mueller report completed**, submitted to DOJ *(not publicly released)*

03/24/19 – TRUMP-RUSSIA INVESTIGATION: Attorney General William **Barr sends 4-page "summary" of Mueller's report to Congress** (made public immediately, intentionally); Barr's conclusions essentially state "no collusion, no obstruction" *(Mueller's team is furious that its report was misrepresented and that Barr refused to release the report's own [accurate] summaries)*

04/18/19 – TRUMP-RUSSIA INVESTIGATION: **Mueller report released publicly**; AG Barr's March 24 "summary" exposed as intentionally misleading (many say, "lying") attempt to create false Trump-exoneration narrative for 25 days to soften impact of Trump's crimes and malfeasance exposed in report

04/25/19 – ELECTION 2020: Joe **Biden announces** candidacy

05/31/19 – MASS SHOOTING: **Virginia Beach**, Va., municipal building; shooter: DeWayne Craddock, 40, Caucasian American terrorist *(12 killed, 4 injured)*

07/24/19 – TRUMP-RUSSIA INVESTIGATION: Special counsel Robert **Mueller testifies before Congress** to: 1) widespread Russian election interference; 2) Trump welcoming, encouraging, using, covering up illegal Russian election help; 3) Trump obstruction of justice during investigation, at least 10 instances *("If the president clearly did not commit a crime, we would have said so")*

07/25/19 – TRUMP EXTORTS UKRAINE: **Trump phone call to extort** Ukrainian President Volodymyr Zelenskyy *(for phony dirt on likely presidential opponent Joe Biden in exchange for already congressionally authorized U.S. military aid to fight off Russian incursion)*

08/03/19 – MASS SHOOTING: **El Paso**, Texas, Walmart retail store; shooter: Patrick Wood Crusius, 21, Caucasian American white supremacist terrorist *(23 killed, 23 injured)*

08/04/19 – MASS SHOOTING: **Dayton**, Ohio, Oregon Historic District; shooter: Connor Betts, 24, Caucasian American terrorist *(9 killed, 17 injured)*

09/01/19 – SHARPIE-GATE: **Trump errs in Hurricane Dorian tweet**; spends 12 days trying to prove he didn't, including redrawing an official weather map with childlike Sharpie markings, which he displayed in news conference

09/24/19 – IMPEACHMENT NO. 1 (EXTORTION OF UKRAINE): House Speaker Nancy Pelosi begins **"official impeachment inquiry"**

09/25/19 – IMPEACHMENT NO. 1 (EXTORTION OF UKRAINE): **Trump releases transcript of call** to Ukrainian President Zelenskyy *(Trump thinks it exonerates him, though clearly it implicates him; he famously asked Zelenskyy, "We'd like you to do us a favor though.")*

12/18/19 – IMPEACHMENT NO. 1 (EXTORTION OF UKRAINE): **House votes to impeach** President Trump *(2 articles)*

12/mid/19 – PANDEMIC: COVID-19 **coronavirus first identified** in Wuhan, China

01/09/20 – HILLARY CLINTON CLEARED OF EVERYTHING: Trump **DOJ clears Hillary Clinton** of all charges, accusations, allegations ever lodged at her *(news is buried)*

01/30/20 – PANDEMIC: **WHO declares "Public Health Emergency** of International Concern"

01/31/20 – PANDEMIC: Trump institutes porous **China travel ban**, follows U.S. airlines and 38 other countries

02/05/20 – IMPEACHMENT NO. 1 (EXTORTION OF UKRAINE): **Senate acquits** President Trump *(1 Republican, Mitt Romney, joins all 47 Democrats in vote to convict, 48-52; 67 were needed)*

02/06/20 – PANDEMIC: **1ˢᵗ U.S. COVID-19 death** *(in northern California)*

03/15/20 – PANDEMIC: Trump institutes nationwide **social distancing guidelines to last 2 weeks** *(critics, scientists, doctors say this should have been done weeks sooner and lasted much longer)*

05/25/20 – BLACK LIVES MATTER: **George Floyd murdered** by on-duty Minneapolis police officer during routine encounter involving minor infraction *(national record-large protests begin over succeeding days including people of all ethnicities)*

05/27/20 – PANDEMIC: **U.S. hits 100,000 COVID-19 deaths;** Trump universally panned for mishandling pandemic; he's played down, belittled, and politicized dangers and refused to nationalize prevention recommendations, supply manufacturing, and supply chain, all in the belief that these moves will hurt economy, thereby hurt his reelection chances *(expert estimates determine Trump malfeasance responsible for half of all U.S. COVID-19 deaths to date)*

06/01/20 – TRUMP BIBLE PHOTO OP: **Trump orders federal forces to clear legal, peaceful D.C. protesters** — using rubber bullets, tear gas, flash-bang shells — for photo op in front of church, to display his "toughness" in handling BLM protests *(Trump is excoriated by multiple top generals, other national luminaries)*

06/05/20 – ELECTION 2020: Joe **Biden clinches Democratic nomination**

07/mid/20 - PANDEMIC: **U.S. hits 150,000 COVID-19 deaths;** expert estimates determine Trump malfeasance responsible for half of all U.S. COVID-19 deaths to date *(U.S.: 4.3% of Earth's population, 22% of its pandemic deaths)*

08/11/20 – ELECTION 2020: Joe **Biden chooses Sen. Kamala Harris (D-Calif.) as vice presidential** running mate

08/18/20 – TRUMP-RUSSIA INVESTIGATION: GOP-controlled **Senate Intelligence Committee report confirms extensive Russian 2016 U.S. election interference, collusion** between Trump campaign and Russia

09/18/20 – SUPREME COURT – Justice **Ruth Bader Ginsburg (liberal) dies** at 87; *(Senate Majority Leader Mitch McConnell, R-Ky., vows to fill seat before election, ignoring "McConnell Rule" established upon Justice Gorsuch's confirmation: no hearings in last year of presidential term)*

09/26/20 – SUPREME COURT: President **Trump nominates Amy Coney Barrett**, Trump's 3rd nominee

10/02/20 – TRUMP CONTRACTS COVID-19: President Trump **hospitalized for 3 days**, leaves hospital against medical advice *(exposes aides, contacts to virus; still plays down dangers, refuses to role-model and nationalize prevention guidelines)*

10/08/20 – KIDNAPPING PLOT – GOV. GRETCHEN WHITMER (D-MICH.): **FBI foiled white supremacist militia plan**, hatched over previous 5 months, to "kidnap … and hold for ransom and reward" the Mich. governor *(white supremacist militia group was angry about state's COVID-19 stay-at-home restrictions, and partially were inspired after President Trump tweeted April 17, 2020: "LIBERATE MINNESOTA! … LIBERATE MICHIGAN! … LIBERATE VIRGINIA, and save your great 2nd Amendment. It is under siege!")*

10/27/20 – SUPREME COURT: **Senate confirms Amy Coney Barrett**, Trump's 3rd justice *(conservative majority now at 6-3)*

11/03/20 – ELECTION DAY: **Joe Biden defeats Donald Trump;** Biden wins Electoral College 306-232; Biden wins popular vote 81.3M-74.2M, 51.3%-46.9% *(results not confirmed for 4 days due to late counting of deluge of Biden-friendly mail-in ballots)*

12/mid/20 – PANDEMIC: **U.S. hits 300,000 COVID-19 deaths;** expert estimates determine Trump malfeasance responsible for half of all U.S. COVID-19 deaths to date *(U.S.: 4.2% of Earth's population, 19% of its pandemic deaths)*

01/06/21 – INSURRECTION OF JANUARY 6: **Trump-supporting seditionists attempt to stop congressional pro forma certification of Electoral College votes** overseen by Vice President Mike Pence *(Trump supporters breach, terrorize, ransack Capitol building for several hours, causing 7 deaths, 140 police injuries; Trump watched on TV, refused to take any action, for approximately 3 hours)*

01/13/21 – IMPEACHMENT NO. 2 (INCITEMENT OF INSURRECTION): **House votes to impeach** President Donald Trump *(1 article)*

01/20/21 – INAUGURATION DAY: Joe **Biden takes office** as 46th president

02/13/21 – IMPEACHMENT NO. 2 (INCITEMENT OF INSURRECTION): **Senate acquits** former President Trump *(7 Republicans join all 50 Democrats in vote to convict, 57-43; 67 were needed)*

02/21/21 – PANDEMIC: **U.S. hits 500,000 COVID-19 deaths;** expert estimates determine Trump malfeasance responsible for half of all U.S. COVID-19 deaths to date *(U.S.: 4.2% of Earth's population, 20% of its pandemic deaths)*

For detailed Trump-Russia timeline, visit:
https://www.factcheck.org/2017/06/timeline-russia-investigation/

"Had racism been toxic to the American electorate, Trump's candidacy would not have been viable."

(Serwer, Adam; "The Nationalist's Delusion"; *The Atlantic;* 11/20/2017.)